D1015678

AMERICAN PROFILES

MILITARY LEADERS OF THE CIVIL WAR

∎

Patrick Austin Tracey

Facts On File

Military Leaders of the Civil War

Copyright © 1993 by Patrick Austin Tracey

All rights reserved. No part of this book may be reproduced or utilized in any form or by any means, electronic or mechanical, including photocopying, recording, or by any information storage or retrieval systems, without permission in writing from the publisher. For information contact:

Facts On File, Inc.
460 Park Avenue South
New York NY 10016

Library of Congress Cataloging-in-Publication Data

Tracey, Patrick.
 Military leaders of the Civil War / Patrick Tracey.
  p. cm. — (American profiles)
 Includes bibliographical references and index.
 Summary: A collection of biographical profiles of eight noted military leaders of the Civil War, including Robert E. Lee, George Henry Thomas, and William Tecumseh Sherman.
 ISBN 0-8160-2671-8 (acid-free paper)
  1. United States—History—Civil War, 1861–1865—Biography—Juvenile literature. 2. Generals—United States—Biography—Juvenile literature. 3. Generals—Confederate States of America—Biography—Juvenile literature. 4. United States. Army—Biography—Juvenile literature. 5. Confederate States of America. Army—Biography—Juvenile literature. [1. United States—History—Civil War, 1861–1865—Biography. 2. Generals.] I. Title.
 II. Series: American profiles (Facts On File, Inc.)
 E467.T73   1993
 973.7'3'0922—dc20   92-34346
 [B]

A British CIP catalogue record for this book is available from the British Library.

Facts On File books are available at special discounts when purchased in bulk quantities for businesses, associations, institutions or sales promotions. Please contact our Special Sales Department in New York at 212/683-2244 (dial 800/322-8755 except in NY).

Series interior by Ron Monteleone
Cover design by F. C. Pusterla Design
Composition by Facts On File, Inc.
Manufactured by the Maple-Vail Book Manufacturing Group
Printed in the United States of America

10 9 8 7 6 5 4 3 2 1

This book is printed on acid-free paper.

920
TRA
1993

Contents

Introduction

Well over a century has passed since the Civil War, but to this day it remains an emotionally charged subject to the American people. The conflict, sometimes known as the War of Secession, and also as the War Between the States, cost 620,000 lives and redefined the meaning of freedom in America.

It was fought between 11 seceding states and the United States government from 1861 to 1865. The basic cause of the struggle was the fact that the United States had since its foundation developed into two distinct sections with different interests. The North was chiefly a manufacturing and commercial region, with small farms, whereas the South was mainly an agricultural region, with large plantations.

For 40 years preceding the war the two regions argued over two issues. One was the question of extension of slavery into the territories of the United States not yet formed into states. The other was the question of states' rights.

The North had far superior material resources than the South, but at the beginning of the war suffered several disadvantages. Not the least of these was the considerable number of U.S. Army officers who came from Southern states who resigned to enter the Confederate army.

The most notable of these officers to resign from the U.S. Army was Colonel Robert E. Lee. He declined Lincoln's offer of the field command of the armies of the North, became commander in chief of the Confederate forces of his native state, Virginia, and molded an outnumbered, outgunned, ragtag army into a fighting force that held the North to a virtual standstill for nearly four years.

Like Lee, the other generals sketched in this book had all graduated from the U.S. Military Academy at West Point, and most, with the exception of the younger officers, fought in the Mexican War. Many of them had been classmates, in fact, and later became brother officers in the United States Army. Now, in the spring of 1861, they would be split between North and South.

iv

Introduction

Many fought strictly by the book, by what they had learned at West Point, never daring to break rules. But the most successful commanders generally achieved their military success by abandoning standard strategies. The one glaring exception in this collection is General George H. Thomas, who had no occasion to adopt unconventional strategies.

What served all of them best, no doubt, was the sheer force of their personalities. All of these leaders had more than their military backgrounds in common; they all possessed the power of their own convictions. Fear of failure or of losing popularity did not enter into their calculations. Their greatest conquests were over themselves.

In the selection of generals made for this book, I have tried to choose among the best leaders and show something of their characters. Each brief biography portrays a general who played a prominent role as an outstanding leader of men. The selections were not restricted to those who commanded armies for a considerable length of time. Nor were admirals chosen. Despite some notable engagements, the naval history of the war was of comparative unimportance.

Finally, many prominent generals who were satisfied with half-measures in battle have been left out. General George B. McClellan of the Northern Army of the Potomac, for example, was a competent enough general who had a major impact on the war, though his inclusion in this book is hardly warranted. McClellan's reluctance to commit troops was starkly revealed at Antietam, when if he had only attacked Lee, the war might have been ended then and there.

It is hoped that this book will bring to life again the personalities of these leading commanders on both sides. Major battles or campaigns are chosen as the high point of each general's military career, with reasons for success or failure emphasized in light of each general's personal nature or disposition.

Each biography is meant to serve as a primer for the lives of these great generals, the times they lived in, and the agonizing choices they made before, during, and after the war. The bibliography following each biography offers additional readings, which young adults are strongly encouraged to explore.

The biographies will appeal to those readers who hold no fixed opinions, who are willing to see the other side of the coin. None of the generals chosen was perfect in all respects, not even Lee, and not all were pure butchers, not even William Tecumseh

Sherman, as many have been led to believe. Confederate James Longstreet was probably too slow and stubborn for his own good, and the impetuosity of the dashing Jeb Stuart did not always serve the Confederacy well.

Nor did war come easy to most of these men. Thomas, who had always regarded himself an orderly man, was now required to witness the disorder of war. Others, like the enigmatic "Stonewall" Jackson, abhorred war as the accumulation of all evils. For Ulysses S. Grant, however, the army was, first and foremost, a good career move. That it was also the vehicle that could save the Union and propel him into the presidency was never his dimmest consideration.

While the defeat of the Confederacy was nearly inevitable, it took much longer than many in the North believed it would at the outset of the hostilities. What ended the bloodiest conflict in American history was the steady determination of men like Grant, Sherman, Thomas, and Phil Sheridan. It was their dogged persistence in battle after battle that finally thinned the Confederate enemy of materials, money, and men.

Each man in this book brought to the war a special quality of leadership that inspired the thousands of foot soldiers who left their houses and farms for years, marched hundreds of miles from home, and charged wildly into the hail of bullets and bayonets awaiting them at each new battlefield. The brilliant daring and genius of Lee is what inspired his rebels to fight against overwhelmingly impossible odds. For Grant, simple common sense, courage, and manliness motivated his men—and paid off handsomely when he finally accomplished what six preceding U.S. generals were unable to do: defeat Lee and bring the South to its knees.

It is hoped that readers will see something new in all of these leaders, making these biographies more than just another rehashing of the Civil War from the traditional military point of view. The collection will be successful if it demonstrates that very few people can succeed in their chosen field unless they are willing to take certain risks and stick to their own convictions.

Robert E. Lee
The Mythical Phoenix

Robert E. Lee
(Library of Congress)

*P*ut yourself in this soldier's shoes: You are a highly decorated colonel on the eve of the War Between the States. The nation's top-ranking general wants you for one of the U.S. Army's most important field commands—the one that is likely to lead to the invasion of your home state of Virginia. This is the dilemma Robert E. Lee found himself in during the weeks before Virginia's

1

secession from the Union. Summoned to Washington, Lee respectfully declined the offer. "Though opposed to secession and deprecating war," he said, "I could take no part in an invasion of the Southern States."

The repercussions of Lee's choice were enormous. Instead of helping to restore the Union, he derailed its mighty war machine. Most Americans know Lee best for his surrender at Appomattox, which brought the Civil War close to its end. But his daring and genius in the face of impossible odds kept the North from capturing the Southern capital of Richmond for four bloody years. Like the mythical phoenix, Lee kept rising from the ashes, even managing to break loose for two invasions of the North. Five years after Appomattox, he died in dignity as the most beloved figure of the Old South.

The youngest of four children, Robert Edward Lee was born on January 9, 1807, in a fine old Southern manor house in Stratford, Virginia. It is not known where he first got the idea of a military profession, but it was definitely in his blood. Lee's father, Henry, was a famous patriot in George Washington's Continental Army. After Washington gave him a cavalry command, he became known as "Light Horse Harry."

Unfortunately, Harry's performance as a father and provider fell short of his military record. Within a few years of his marriage to Anne Hill Carter, he squandered her personal fortune on some bad investments that left his wife and three children destitute. Anne suffered from a crippling arthritis for most of her adult life. And as Harry's fortunes declined, her health deteriorated.

Lee's mother nearly died from his birth. She recovered, only to see Harry sent to debtors' prison two years later. When Harry was released, Anne moved the family to Alexandria, Virginia. Today Alexandria is a charming suburban town seven miles downriver from the nation's capital. In the early 19th century, it was a bustling commercial center, with the largest seaport on the east coast.

Anne Lee said she was moving there to find better schools for her children, but she may have had other motives. Alexandria also was home to Harry's two brothers and his sister. Anne may have hoped their stabilizing influence would give the family a more settled life.

Any hopes for Harry's reform vanished quickly. Within a couple of years, Harry was almost fatally injured in a brawl in Baltimore. Robert was five years old when his father was brought home in the winter of 1813. Harry's moods were as ill as his health then, and his bursts of rage echoed through the Lee house for months. By spring, though, he had gone to Barbados in search of a better climate, saying he would be back soon. That was the last that Robert ever saw of him. Light Horse Harry died on his way home from the West Indies in 1818.

With Harry's absence, Lee's mother was the biggest influence in young Robert's life. Anne Lee was an invalid for most of her adult life. Because her oldest son, Carter, was away at Harvard when Harry died, it fell to Robert to take care of her. Robert could often be seen carrying her out to the family horse carriage. On these carriage rides, he kept her entertained with his cheerful sense of humor. When she complained about the cold, Robert jokingly fashioned a makeshift curtain out of an old newspaper and used it to keep the wind from whistling into the crevices of the old family coach.

After school, when other boys went off to play, Lee marched straight home to administer his mother's medicine. At such a young age, Lee was shouldering a responsibility that probably instilled the sense of self-sacrifice he exhibited throughout his life. But there's no doubt he missed out on a lot of the fun of boyish mischiefs.

With his father out of the picture, Robert found a better male role model in none other than the legendary George Washington. Although the father of the nation had died eight years before Lee's birth, his spirit was believed to watch over the country from the shadows of his estate at Mount Vernon. Mount Vernon was only an hour's carriage ride from Alexandria, and the Lee and Washington families were close friends.

Every week Robert and his mother heard scripture read from Washington's bible at the Old Christ Church. Robert also heard tales of General Washington from many of the local tradesmen who were proud of having served in his Continental Army. All of this made Washington a living presence to Lee.

Lee was a good student at the Alexandria Academy. His teacher said he always finished his assignments with careful attention to detail. After high school, however, college was out of the question because of his mother's dwindling bank account. So Robert applied to West Point and was accepted in 1824. Lee's mother was wheeled to the train station to see him off. Neither was given to public displays of emotion, but the parting was hard for both of them. Only after Robert left did Mrs. Lee turn to her sister-in-law and sob, "How can I live without Robert? He is both a son and a daughter to me."

Lee enjoyed the routine of West Point and continued to be a good scholar. He never smoked or drank, and he refrained from the pranks and practical jokes pulled by the other cadets. Not that Lee was at all unpopular. He was very well liked for his gentle sense of humor, which gave a light turn to conversation, but he was not a social mixer. By nature, or perhaps deriving from the stoical discipline instilled in him as a boy, what Lee liked best was steady work. Passing the hours in solitary attention to his studies gave him peace of mind. These powers of concentration paid off when he was graduated second in the exceptionally brilliant West Point class of 1829.

Lee cut a handsome figure in his gray cadet uniform. By the time of his second-year furlough from West Point, he had grown tall. Not surprisingly, he caught the eye of Mary Anne Randolph Custis. Mary and Robert had actually known each other since childhood. They had met when Lee was a boy going on fox hunts at her father's estate. The childhood friendship blossomed into love, and the two were married in 1831.

Mary's father, George Washington Parke Custis, was the adopted son of George and Martha Washington. He built Arlington, a sprawling estate with huge palisade timbers, rising up from the banks of the Potomac River. Arlington housed many of the paintings and Revolutionary War relics that belonged to George Washington. By his marriage to Mary Custis, Lee became direct heir to Washington's estate. Lee could not have been unaware, as a friend said, that marrying Mary "in the eyes of the world" also would make him "the representative of the founder of American liberty."

In 1831, Lee took his first post as second lieutenant, helping shore up seawall escarpments on Chesapeake Bay. Mary joined him there. They shared a house near Fort Monroe and she became pregnant with their first child. But she didn't last long at Fort Monroe. Like Lee's mother Anne, Mary suffered from a crippling illness as an adult. Besides, she preferred the beauty and serenity of Arlington to the hardships of military life. The two lived apart for most of Lee's career. At Arlington, which Lee tried to visit every Christmas, they had seven children in rapid succession, despite Mary's severe rheumatism.

In 1835, Lee moved back to Arlington and served as assistant to the chief of army engineers in Washington. The following spring he was sent to the vast northwest region of the country, now the Midwest, where he helped settle a dispute between Ohio and Michigan over their state border on Lake Erie. Late in 1837, he went to St. Louis to oversee the rechanneling of the Mississippi River.

Mary joined Robert in St. Louis in the spring of 1838. By this time they had two daughters. A year later, however, Mary and the children returned to Arlington. Lee began to grow lonely. His heart was not in his work. His schedule dragged and the Army pay was poor. His malaise deepened after a tour inspecting forts in the Carolinas in April of 1841.

Lee persevered in spite of his dissatisfaction with military life, following his career to Fort Hamilton in New York. Fort Hamilton was located on the Brooklyn side of the Narrows of New York Harbor. It was close enough for Lee to travel several times a year to Arlington. But he was still weary of the army. The work, which consisted of shoring up rotting defense works, continued to bore him.

Lee finally saw his first military action after Congress declared war on Mexico on May 9, 1846. He began as a captain of engineers before joining the command of General Winfield Scott one month later. In one campaign, at Cerro Gordo, Lee made a daring night-time expedition that Scott called "the greatest feat of physical and moral courage" of the entire war.

Several other staff officers had been dispatched to scout around the enemy flanks so that Scott would know where to position his troops. The mission called for a night-time expedition across a slippery tract of rocks known as the Pedegral. Several teams returned to report that the Pedegral was impossible to cross. So Lee went alone, crossing the Pedegral in daylight, then returning at night by torchlight. Lee's expedition opened the way for the eventual invasion of Mexico City. General Scott later called him "the very best soldier that I ever saw in the field."

After the Mexican War was won, Lee returned to the States as a brevet colonel, which was a promotion in rank but not in pay or authority. In 1852 he was appointed superintendent of the West Point Military Academy. Anne's rheumatism kept her confined, but Lee and his children often skated on the frozen Hudson River in the wintertime.

Lee was credited with improving the academy, but he was not fulfilled there. He still longed for the glory he had experienced in the Mexican War. In 1855, he jumped at the chance to join a cavalry regiment Congress had formed for the army. When he left for Fort Mason, Texas, his family returned to Arlington. Lee had been picked for the cavalry regiment after Secretary of War Jefferson Davis had decided it was "time to see the son of Light Horse Harry in the saddle."

Lee returned from Texas for a brief period in 1859 to help settle his father-in-law's estate. Two hundred slaves had remained at Arlington, and Lee wrote to one of his sons that there was some trouble when "some of the people . . . rebelled against my authority, refused to obey my orders, and said they were as free as I was." Lee said he "succeeded in capturing them, however, tied them, and lodged them in jail."

The story made the rounds with various changes. Lee found himself appearing in the Northern newspapers as a vicious brute who whipped slaves mercilessly. "The New York Tribune attacked me for my treatment of your father's slaves, but I shall not reply," Lee wrote to his wife Mary from Texas. "He has left me an unpleasant legacy."

Like other Southerners who were basically against slavery, Lee urged gradual abolition. For the most part, he was concerned with how freed slaves would support themselves. Although he acknowledged it was unfeasible, Lee said his first instinct "would be to free all the slaves and send them to Liberia, to their native land."

The slave issue would touch Lee personally once more before the end of 1859. In October, a famous but foolhardy white abolitionist named John Brown had raided an armory at Harpers Ferry, Virginia. Brown was holed up with 13 hostages in an engine firehouse when Lee was called upon to arrest him.

Lee's marines stormed the firehouse and captured Brown with little w__te of time. Afterwards Lee returned to his post in Texas. But the John Brown episode was just one of the many forewarnings of war that were occurring all over the country. Apart from the slavery issue, the United States was divided by issues as unsettling and unwieldy as states' rights and industrialization. Lee said he resented "the aggressions" of Northern states against the South, but he was "not pleased with the course of the Cotton States as they call themselves."

A year later he would have to take a stand. In February of 1861, Texas became the seventh state to secede from the United States. Lee was summoned to Washington by General Winfield Scott. Lee's commander in Mexico, Scott was now the highest-ranking general in the army.

Everyone at Fort Mason assumed Scott would offer Lee the command of a Union army. As Lee said goodbye, one of his cavalry officers called out, "Colonel, do you intend to go South or remain North?" The officers strained to hear Lee's response. "I shall never bear arms against the Union," he answered. "But," he added, "it may be necessary for me to carry a musket in defense of my native state, Virginia."

Lee met with Scott in Washington and declined the command of the army intended for the invasion of the South. He then crossed over the Potomac River and returned to his family at Arlington. Back home, Lee was the toast of the town. Everywhere he went people were referring to him as the "second Washington." Lee actually believed he was doing as Washington would have done. After all, Lee surmised, the republic was founded by people like Washington, who were absolutely committed to states' rights.

When Virginia seceded, Lee became commander of the state's armed forces. Weeks later, when the state joined the Confederacy, he was appointed to organize the Southern troops arriving in Richmond. Soon he was asked to become military adviser to Confederate President Jefferson Davis. Although it was primarily an office job, Lee accepted the position without complaint.

Not until the autumn of 1861 did Lee see battle. Davis sent him to western Virginia to help fight Union forces in the Shenandoah Valley. It was an unsuccessful campaign, its failure caused mainly by the incompetence of two sparring Confederate officers. Disgruntled newspaper editors, who had come to expect much of the son of Light Horse Harry Lee, began to question his military skills, dubbing him "Granny Lee."

Lee ignored the bad press. He enjoyed the faith of President Davis, who toward the end of the year sent Lee to help fortify the South's seacoast defenses in South Carolina, Georgia and Florida. The assignment required the building of earthen defense works against the Union navy. Again, caustic editorials were penned, saying Lee would be better at wielding a spade than a sword. The press now called him "King of Spades."

Halfway through 1862, Lee was given one of the most important jobs in the Confederacy—the command of the Army of Northern Virginia. "Evacuating Lee, who has never yet risked a single battle with the invader," sneered *The Richmond Examiner*. Lee chose not to respond, ignoring the criticism.

Lee and everybody else knew that the Union General George B. McClellan might invade and occupy Richmond, possibly ending the war right there. But it soon became evident that the King of Spades did not intend to hunker down for a siege by McClellan. On the contrary, he told Davis, only a quarter of his army would stay in the trenches protecting Richmond. The rest would attack the approaching Army of the Potomac.

It was a great gamble, leaving it to chance that McClellan would not attack. But Lee was always one to take chances. He took them in the hopes of getting the North to sign a peace treaty early in the war. Otherwise, the South could never outlast the industrialized armies of the North.

Lee weighed the odds, though, before diving into the Seven Days battle. He read the Northern papers avidly. He questioned prisoners on occasion. He knew that McClellan always believed himself outnumbered and was reluctant to attack. So he sent three divisions against McClellan's flank on the other side of the Chickahominy River.

Lee's orders got botched up over a mistake as to the line of the enemy's retreat. At Fraysers Farm, where two converging columns failed to arrive, Lee had hoped to envelope and destroy McClellan. Instead there was an indecisive battle. Lee then prepared another assault. Leaving less than a third of his men in Richmond, he ordered those with him to act aggressively in attack formations. The gray-coated thespians marched back and forth, firing salvos and probing Union defenses. McClellan was puzzled. When he hesitated, Lee's army went after him.

Lee's army met fierce fighting at Malvern Hill. The inexperience of the staff prevented the massing of the whole army in a tangled terrain for a simultaneous attack on the strong Union positions. Isolated attacks failed to dislodge McCellan. But once again, McClellan lost his nerve. Withdrawing that night unchallenged, he took refuge under the gunboats at Harrison's Landing.

The campaign was the most important period in Lee's military education. It taught him the necessity of simpler methods and organization. But Lee's gamble in splitting his army had paid off. It served his immediate purpose in relieving the threat to Richmond. McClellan never did go on the offensive. It was Lee's first victory—an underdog victory at that. He had finally served notice that he was a force to be reckoned with. Newspaper editors gave him a worthier new nickname: the Old Gray Fox.

McClellan withdrew all the way to the Potomac, hoping to hook up with Union Major General John Pope. Lee knew his Army of Northern Virginia was in a dangerous position between Pope and

McClellan, especially if the two were going to unite. So he divided his army again and set a trap. Behind Pope, Lee sent his very best warrior, a fire-and-brimstone Episcopalian preacher named Thomas "Stonewall" Jackson. Following Jackson, Lee sent another force commanded by General James Longstreet.

Jackson smashed Pope's communications lines and slipped away unharmed before Pope and McClellan could unite. While Pope marched for two days in August looking for Jackson, he ran right into Lee's trap—Longstreet's forces at Manassas. Jackson and Longstreet attacked Pope from both sides, and the Union general beat a bewildered retreat to Washington.

The South was jubilant. Lee, by daring and rapid maneuvers, had trounced Pope's much bigger army in the presence of the separate but even larger Army of the Potomac. Lee was lauded as the savior of the South. But he wasn't optimistic about the chances of the South's survival.

While his rebels rejoiced, Lee looked northward to Washington. He knew there was little chance of capturing the heavily-defended Union capital. But he thought he could at least threaten it and thereby force the North to sign a peace treaty. The following month, Lee and 55,000 graycoats waded across the Potomac River and into Maryland.

Lee's first order upon crossing was that there was to be no pillaging and no harm done to innocent civilians. Then he did what he'd always done. He divided his army in half, confident McClellan would be too slow to respond. McClellan was slow in reaching Frederick alright, but there he had an incredible stroke of luck along the way. In an abandoned camp, a package of cigars was found wrapped in a copy of Lee's orders.

It was a golden opportunity for the Union commander. As he told one of his generals, "Here is a paper with which if I cannot whip Bobby Lee, I will be willing to go home." Armed with his cigar wrapper, McClellan pinned down the Army of Northern Virginia at Antietam Creek.

Lee proved to be a great horse soldier, riding along the battle lines and personally directing his troops. It meant a lot to his men that Lee was willing to risk his own life. His rebels knew this about him and loved him for it. A single word from Marse, or Uncle, Robert, as they affectionately called him, could inspire them to almost superhuman feats. But they didn't want him to get killed for it.

"Marse Robert," the horse soldier
(Library of Congress)

At one point, when terrible disaster seemed imminent, Lee rode to the front of the Forty-Ninth Virginia Regiment, quietly took off his hat, and knelt by his faithful warhorse Traveler. To his foot soldiers it was obvious that Lee meant to lead the charge himself. A murmur of disapproval swept through the regiment. Lee's soldiers refused to go forward if it meant risking the life of their brilliant commander.

Just then General John B. Gordon, one of Lee's strongest fighters, appeared at his side. Gordon seized Lee's reins, pleading with him to go to the rear of the battle. Then a rebel's voice boomed out, "General Lee to the rear! We always try to do just what General Gordon tells us, and we will drive them back if General Lee will only go to the rear." As two soldiers took Lee's horse away, Gordon led the charge, exclaiming, "Forward! Charge! And remember your promise to General Lee." The results were telling. The Confederate troops swept forward and pushed back five times their number.

That night Lee met his generals in his tent and listened to their grisly reports. More than a quarter of his men lay dead. The entire day's battle at Antietam marked the bloodiest day in American history. Soldiers later swore it was impossible to move without stepping on a dead or wounded man, Union and Confederate alike. The Army of Northern Virginia was now about a third the size of McClellan's army, and so badly straggling that it was forced to give up the offensive.

Lee's generals had one thing in mind—retreat. But Lee never flinched. As his boyhood teacher had noted, Lee always showed patience in finishing up his assignments, and he meant to wait patiently for McClellan. The attack never came. Apparently, the carnage had shaken McClellan to his boots. That night the army of Northern Virginia built campfires, left them burning, and slipped back across the Potomac to nurse their wounds in the South.

Antietam was tactically a draw, but the fact that Lee was forced to call off the invasion of the North made it a turning point in the war. Though Lee's army had held off against McClellan, it had not pushed close enough to Washington to shake Northern confidence in the administration of President Abraham Lincoln. Lee was tortured by the loss. A month later, he offered his resignation to President Davis.

Davis declined Lee's resignation, but Lee's mood grew gloomier. One of the worst winters in Virginia history was spent with his army in Richmond. His rebels were starving and freezing in their blood-soaked rags. But soldiers reared on stories of Valley Forge drew parallels between themselves and George Washington's Continental Army. If General Washington had rallied against the well-outfitted British, then their beloved Marse Robert could lick the better-equipped Union armies.

Spring finally broke in April of 1863. Union General "Fighting Joe" Hooker crossed into Virginia, boasting to his men about crushing "the finest army on the planet." Hooker headed for Fredericksburg with a force of 180,000, three times the size of Lee's army. While Hooker was advancing straight into the Wilderness, a confusing jungle of scrub timber, Lee was planning to capitalize on the rough terrain, poor visibility, and the element of surprise.

Leaving a small force to hold the heights at Fredericksburg, Lee started west to pounce on Hooker at a pillared brick mansion known as Chancellorsville. Once again, he split his forces. He sent Stonewall Jackson to catch Hooker on his weak right flank. The other third of Lee's rebels were sent against Hooker's left. Hooker thought Lee was retreating. It was a grave miscalculation. From out of nowhere, Jackson crushed Hooker's right side near the Chancellorsville mansion. Lee then prepared for a full-scale attack, but Hooker turned and ran.

Lee had decisively beaten an enemy three times his size. Nothing, it seemed, could break the charm of his invincibility. But he couldn't savor the victory for long. Riding back from Chancellorsville, Stonewall Jackson was mistakenly shot dead in a bizarre and tragic ambush by his own men. Lee had lost his greatest warrior.

If Chancellorsville was Lee's most successful battle, Gettysburg, two months later, was clearly his worst failure. It was Lee's second invasion of the North. His graycoats crossed the Potomac without any trouble, and a series of odd twists led advance units of his army to the quiet little Pennsylvania market town. By the time Lee arrived, his army was spread too far out for him to personally direct the battle lines. Lee was left without the eyes and ears of his army, almost totally ignorant of what the enemy was doing.

On the third day, Lee ordered 15,000 of his men to take a hill known as Cemetery Ridge. His subordinates argued vehemently against the attack. They knew it was dangerous, in light of the fact that Union General George B. Meade held the high ground on Cemetery Ridge. Lee could have chosen to maneuver the Yankees out of the heights, but he insisted on taking the offensive.

As Lee watched from a nearby hill, Confederate Major General George Pickett began a 20-minute assault known as Pickett's Charge. At Cemetery Ridge, Pickett's gunners, and then gunners on both sides, opened fire in the greatest artillery bombardment ever witnessed on the American continent. An ensuing silence seemed to signal that the Confederates should renew their attack. Lee ordered them forward, and then the Union artillery opened fire again, mowing down over 5,000 of Pickett's men—almost half the Confederates on the battlefield—in a vicious slaughter.

Heading back into the South was out of the question, since the Potomac River was too high to cross. "It is all my fault," Lee told his ragged veterans as he rode among them. "All good men must rally." Rally they did, with their backs against the rising river. But the Army of the Potomac never pursued them. When the river fell,

Lee crossed back into Virginia, spared once again from the jaws of defeat.

By 1864, the Union forces had had just about enough of Robert E. Lee. Union General Ulysses S. Grant devised a grand strategy. He would mass three armies and lead the chase himself. Grant then told Lincoln: "Whatever happens, there will be no turning back," until Lee was dislodged from Richmond.

The armies of the Potomac and of Northern Virginia wintered a few miles apart, on both sides of the Rapidan River near Fredericksburg, Virginia. As the dogwood bloomed, Grant prepared to cross. Outnumbered two to one, Lee decided not to contest the river. Instead he chose to hit Grant's bluecoats when they reached the Wilderness, the same confusing woods where Lee had his greatest victory a year earlier against Hooker, at Chancellorsville. There the Union's numerical advantage would count for less.

Lee's army slammed Grant's forces at the Wilderness with the very same tactics that had worked so well against Hooker. But unlike Hooker and McClellan, Grant would not retreat against Lee. He meant to keep his promise to Lincoln, and pushed on. For the first time in a Virginia campaign, the Army of the Potomac stayed on the offensive after its initial battle.

Lee was forced to retreat. He was nothing if not a great defensive strategist, and he continually sideslipped to escape Grant. He ordered his men to build elaborate defensive works wherever they went. After months of skirmishes, Lee's exhausted army dug in at Petersburg below Richmond.

Divining his end, Lee wrote to President Davis that the Confederates would have to concentrate their forces for a last-ditch stand. In February 1865, the Confederate Congress conferred supreme command of all Confederate armies on Lee. But he could no longer control events. The Confederate armies were poorly supplied, and the Southern economy was in a shambles.

Grant broke the Confederate line on April 2. Lee struck out and raced toward the Danville Railroad, but Grant had him in the open at last. Along an obscure stream named Sayler's Creek, three Union divisions cut off a quarter of Lee's army, captured 6,000 rebels and destroyed much of their wagon train. "My God!" exclaimed Lee when he learned of what happened. "Has the army been dissolved?"

Lee's rations had run out. He was outnumbered five to one. The rebels who had been so willing to lay down their lives for Marse Robert began to fall behind and desert in droves. With a heavy heart, Lee sent a soldier riding out across the lines with a white flag of surrender. On April 9, Lee and Grant met in the parlor of Wilmer McLean at Appomattox Courthouse.

The contrast between victor and vanquished could not have been greater. While Lee was tall and handsome, Grant was short and scrappy. Grant walked into the parlor room with mud-spattered trousers tucked into his dirty boots. Lee strode in wearing his full general's uniform, which he seldom wore. A gold sash was wrapped around his shoulder and the jeweled sword of George Washington was tucked into his belt. The two generals shook hands and sat at two separate tables, the two central figures in one of the great tableaus of American history.

Three days after Lee signed the surrender, his ragged Confederates broke ranks and began trudging home. Within three months, all hostilities had ceased. Lee had become the mainstay of the Southern war effort, and when he fell, the whole Confederacy quickly collapsed around him.

After the war, Lee returned to his family in Richmond. The estate at Arlington had been confiscated by the federal government and turned into a military cemetery. In September, he accepted an appointment as president of Washington College in Lexington, Virginia. There, with official status as a paroled prisoner of war, he quietly counseled acceptance by the South of its defeat, and restoration of the Union.

Generals Lee and Grant (General Sheridan between them) discuss terms of surrender at Appomattox Courthouse.
(Library of Congress)

Lee did everything he could to stay out of the public eye. There is no doubt that he wanted to live out his final years within his family circle, and with his invalid wife, Mary Custis, to whom he gave constant care and attention. Lee also knew that his name had become synonymous with the Southern effort, and he wanted the South to look forward and not back. He did not want glory and applause. He wanted to close the door forever on one of the most terrible and agonizing periods in American history.

Lee died from a heart attack at Washington College on October 12, 1870, five years after his defeat. The college subsequently changed its name to Washington and Lee University. Congress never answered his application for amnesty and pardon. In fact, it wasn't until 1975 that Lee's citizenship was restored by an act of Congress.

Lee's funeral service was full of tearful eulogies to a man whose personal virtues were as remarkable as his genius as a man of arms. The public mourning was almost as widespread in the North and in Europe as it was in the South. Editorial writers who were once so quick to criticize him now recalled his nobility as a soldier and citizen.

Military historians have criticized Lee for his defeat at Gettysburg. Some say the suicidal slaughter Lee invited at Cemetery Ridge showed that he did not understand the ravages of modern artillery. They have also questioned why he permitted his troops to be scattered over such a wide area at Gettysburg. Joseph Mitchell explains that Lee "thought he was facing, as always before, an enemy much larger than his own. The way to defeat that army was to fight it in detail until it had been reduced to a strength he could combat on fairly equal terms."

The popular Civil War historian Bruce Catton points out that Lee "was never really beaten in a fair fight. He was foiled, perhaps, though only when the cards were marked at Appomattox and the deck was impossibly stacked with Union forces greatly outnumbering his own." Until then, he continually frustrated Union invasions with slick defensive maneuvers and stinging counterattacks. Almost invariably, he bested his enemy with fewer soldiers and smaller resources.

With the exception of Gettysburg, Lee was the living emblem of military perfection, a master of defensive and offensive tactics. But if Lee was such a genius, why did the South lose? "The North had a potential manpower superiority of more than three to one and Union armed forces had an actual superiority of two to one during most of the war," says historian James McPherson. "In economic resources and logistical capacity the northern advantage was even greater. Thus, in this explanation, the Confederacy fought against overwhelming odds; its defeat was inevitable."

Chronology

January 19, 1807	born in Stratford, Virginia
July 1829	graduates West Point
May 1831	serves at Fort Monroe, Virginia
May 30, 1831	marries Mary Ann Randolph Custis
1834	assistant to chief of army engineers
1835	aided in running Ohio-Michigan
1836	made first lieutenant of Engineers
July 1837	superintendent for St. Louis Harbor
1838	promoted to captain
October 1841	transferred to Fort Hamilton
August 19, 1846	sent to San Antonio as army assistant engineer
September 13, 1847	wounded in Mexican War at Chapultec
1848	promoted to brevet colonel
November 1848	transferred to Fort Carroll, Maryland
August 1852	superintendent at West Point
March 1855	made lieutenant colonel
1859	captured John Brown at Harpers Ferry
March 16, 1861	made colonel of 1st Cavalry
April 25, 1861	resigns from U.S. Army
June 14, 1861	promoted to general, CSA
May 31, 1862	assigned to command Army of Northern Virginia
June 1862	Seven Days' Battle
August 30, 1862	battle of Second Manassas
September 17, 1862	battle of Antietam
December 13, 1862	battle of Fredericksburg
May 6, 1863	battle of Chancellorsville

Military Leaders of the Civil War

July 2, 1863	battle of Gettysburg
May 8–21, 1864	battle of Spotsylvania
June 3, 1864	battle of Cold Harbor
February 6, 1865	designated general in chief of Confederate armies
April 9, 1865	surrenders to Grant at Appomattox Courthouse
June 13, 1865	applies for pardon
October 12, 1870	dies in Lexington, Virginia

Further Reading

Jones, J. William. *Personal Reminiscences of General Robert E. Lee*. Richmond: United States Historical Society Press, 1989. Stresses Lee's devotion to duty, giving equal footing to his genius as a general and his emergence as a national figure unpoisoned by bitterness.

Meridith, Roy. *The Face of Robert E. Lee in Life and in Legend*. New York: Fairfax Press; distributed by Crown Publishers, 1981. A solid biography of Lee for popular audiences.

Pennington, Estill Curtis. *The Last Meeting's Lost Cause*. Spartanburg, South Carolina: R. M. Hicklin, 1988. A well-researched and balanced view of Lee and his decision to surrender at Appomattox.

Smith, Gene. *Lee and Grant*. New York: Meridian, 1984. An extremely well-written dual biography of Grant and Lee.

ALBUQUERQUE ACADEMY LIBRARY

George Henry Thomas
"The Rock of Chickamauga"

George Henry Thomas
(Library of Congress)

*M*ost of the generals on both sides of the Civil War could have afforded to lose a battle or two without the risk of tarnishing their reputations. George Henry Thomas could not. Thomas was a Southerner who chose to fight with the North. Because of his background, many Northerners suspected that he was secretly bound to his secessionist home state of Virginia. Even after he had proven himself among the ablest of Union generals, with a growing reputation as an imperturbable master of conventional tactics and strategy, his loyalty was still called into question.

It was ironic that Thomas was eyed with suspicion, for, in spite of his Southern birth, he never doubted his own loyalty to the Union. He had carefully studied the Constitution of the United States and was a firm believer in the ideas upon which the federal government was based. From the first outbreak of rebellion, he upheld his allegiance to the United States flag.

It is not surprising, given his sensitive position, that Thomas was a general who fought "by the book." If at any time he had lost a battle, and he never did, he could have expected to be fired. There was, in any case, no occasion for him to deviate from conventional military tactics. Great boldness was never expected of him. Except at the battle of Chickamauga, his forces always outnumbered the enemy's.

George Henry Thomas was born on July 31, 1816. The fourth of nine children, he had six sisters and two brothers. The family homestead was near Newsom's Depot in Virginia, five miles from the North Carolina line, in Southampton County, which forms the watershed between the James River and the streams that flow into North Carolina's Albemarle Sound.

Thomas was descended on his father's side from Welsh ancestry, and on his mother's from a French Huguenot family. His family was better off than ordinary Virginians, and were among the most respected of Virginia farmers. His early home life was pleasant and content. George had a knack for mastering all the subjects he studied in the local Southampton Academy, which was one of the finest schools the region had to offer.

But he was a disobedient child. As a young boy, he seemed to prefer the company of his family's slaves. Against his parents' wishes, he spent time teaching the slave children to read the lessons he had learned at church and school. When he visited the slave quarters, he would often swap sugar he had pilfered for raccoon and possum skins.

When George was only 16 years old his father died from a farming accident. As the oldest boy, George then began to manage the farm. But he had never liked farm work. Whenever he could, he would visit the local saddler's shop to learn how to make his own saddles, or he would go to the cabinetmaker's for lessons in making furniture.

With little or no parental direction, George kept himself busy throughout his adolescence. At age 19, he began the study of law while serving as assistant to his uncle, James Rochelle, clerk of the county court in nearby Jerusalem. One day in the early spring of 1836, the congressman of the district, John Young Mason, called at Rochelle's office and let it be known that he had an appointment to fill at the United States Military Academy at West Point.

Thomas arrived at the academy several weeks early to brush up on his studies. He was approaching his 20th birthday and was two years older than most of his classmates. He bore a robust physical presence, being six feet in height and weighing about 200 pounds. His fellow cadets, who noticed a resemblance in him to another large figure in American history, nicknamed him George Washington.

Thomas was a hard-working student who left nothing undone from his assignments. He preferred the scientific subjects, especially geology, which he studied during his last two years at the academy. Rising steadily in rank, he went from 26th in his class at the end of his first year to 12th in a class of 42 at graduation. In 1840, he received his diploma and a second lieutenant's commission, bid farewell to his classmates, and went back to Virginia on leave.

Soon he was assigned to the Third Artillery at Fort Columbus, in New York Harbor. There four companies were being recruited for service in Florida, a perennial Indian battleground since Andrew Jackson's invasion of the peninsula in 1818. Like most graduating West Pointers, Thomas was chafing for action, with no real war in sight. In November he left for Savannah, Georgia, where he set sail for Fort Lauderdale.

Fort Lauderdale was then a shabby little garrison about 200 feet from the ocean. Behind it ran a deep and slow-moving river. Farther back lay a jungle of swamp cypress and tropical growth. The buzzing of mosquitoes and other winged insects was unceasing.

Thomas devoted much of his time to the quest for supplies, hunting in the swampy jungle for wild turkey and deer. Since he proved unusually attentive to the task, he was made quartermaster. It was a dreary assignment that kept him confined to the vicinity of the camp. Other officers had the more exciting job of skirmishing with small bands of Seminole Indians.

After nearly a year of wrestling with problems of supply and demand, Thomas received an assignment that raised his spirits. Ordered to navigate a river and ransack some of its native villages, he set off with a detachment of 60 men. After most of the Seminoles had fled inland to the safety of the Everglades, Thomas received a brevet for bravery.

Sometime during December, Thomas sailed around the peninsula to army headquarters at the head of Tampa Bay, and in early February he made off for New Orleans. The city's wharves were crowded with transport ships, its streets filled each night with drunken soldiers celebrating the close of the campaigns against the Indians. In July of 1842, with the thermometer rising well into the 90s, Thomas was pleased to leave when the regiment was ordered to sail for the city of Charleston, South Carolina.

His new post, Fort Moultrie, was on Sullivan's Island, a fine summer resort area for the prominent families of Charleston. Across the harbor Thomas could see ships dumping ballast for the foundation of Fort Sumter. Twenty years later, every available man in Charleston Harbor would be called to its defense on the eve of the Civil War.

At Fort Moultrie, many Charleston socialites were honored dinner guests, and they brought their secessionist ideas with them. But Thomas's superiors had issued a warning to keep tongues checked. Thomas, who was known for his keen sense of humor, kept on guard whenever political arguments heated up.

Leave from Fort Moultrie came after the customary two-year interval. Thomas was transferred in November to Fort McHenry on Whetstone Point near Baltimore. Here, too, there was much gaiety and social life in the nearby city, and many West Pointers found themselves in demand at masquerade parties and balls. But service at Fort McHenry was not prolonged. Within a year and after promotion to first lieutenant, Thomas was transferred back to Fort Moultrie.

At that time, there were signs of an approaching war with Mexico. In the autumn of 1845, he joined the command of General Zachary Taylor, an old Indian fighter from the Florida campaigns. With Taylor's forces, Thomas set out early the next year for the valley of the muddy Rio Grande. When his company arrived in the port city of Corpus Christi, they were the first U.S. troops to occupy the soil of Texas. Annexation of independent Texas by the United States had already been agreed to by the Texas Congress and ratified by the people of that republic. Thomas found himself caught up in the march of events when orders came to Taylor to start southward for the Rio Grande early in February 1846.

On the north bank of the river Thomas helped build a massive six-sided garrison, which was christened Fort Texas. He soon saw a burst of energy among the artillerymen at Fort Texas as the first shots were exchanged with General Mariano Arista across the river. Thomas worked his own gun sparingly. The Mexican redoubts were difficult to hit, and he wished to reserve his store of shells for a later day.

Five days later, he joined with Taylor as the Americans battered their way through Arista's advance line at Palo Alto. The next day, at Resaca de la Palma in Cameron County, he still had a supply of shells stacked up, and lobbed them at the fleeing Mexicans as they sped homeward across the river.

Two days later Thomas and his company crossed into Matamoros. Placed in command of two 12-inch fieldpieces, he marched ahead with some regulars and a company of Texans, who met little resistance. In a desolate spot called Camargo, one of the hottest places in the entire region, he was selected to join the advance to Monterrey, 100 miles to the southwest.

Two weeks of marching with his company under Captain Braxton Bragg brought Thomas within sight of the soaring cathedral towers of Monterrey. An immense fortification known as the Citadel guarded the approaches to the city, while Mexican sharpshooters swarmed over the housetops and roof of the cathedral. Thomas banged away with his guns, creating a diversion while others detoured to cut off the main supply route to the south.

Fighting began on the streets of the city the next day. In the afternoon, Thomas and his men were pent up in a narrow alley between the walls of two adobe houses. Bullets were showering down on them. Some men were badly hit. Four horses were killed and several wounded. Ordered to retreat, Thomas reloaded one more time and gave the enemy a parting shot. He managed to hold them off until horses arrived to haul away his gun carriage, then he shot his way to safety and helped drive the Mexicans from the plaza and the rooftops. For this display of gallantry under fire, Thomas was promoted to brevet captain.

The road now led south to Buena Vista. There General Lopez de Santa Anna, the former Mexican president and now the commander of Mexican forces, led a charge against the American invaders. Thomas was left almost alone on a bare plateau as the enemy approached. He was under fire for more than eight hours.

Still, he held his ground, firing artillery at the bloodstained Mexican columns. Finally, the charge faltered. The enemy fell back in defeat.

Thomas was named a brevet major for his bravery at Buena Vista. Back home, a public meeting of Southampton County citizens passed a resolution praising Thomas for his bravery and military skill. A collection was taken up for a handsomely decorated gift sword, its scabbard beautifully engraved with a vignette of Monterrey.

In August of 1848, the U.S. Army returned across the Rio Grande into a much expanded U.S.A. But Thomas was not among his fellow veterans. He remained in Mexico for another six months, at Brazos Santiago near the mouth of the river, as part of a force selected to occupy the conquered country. Among the first to enter Mexico, he was now among the last to leave. Late in February he returned home to his Virginia farmhouse.

He was not there very long before the call went out for troops to serve again in Florida. The Indians there were becoming rebellious again, and Thomas was recruited to help with the suppression because of his experience. Early in 1853, however, an artillery instructor's position opened at West Point. Thomas received the appointment in March and returned on short notice to the familiar scenes on the west bank of the Hudson River.

At West Point he received the additional duty of cavalry instructor. Weighing 200 pounds, he was a little too heavy to be the ideal cavalry commander, although this was the branch of the service he loved most. In fact, West Point cadets dubbed him "Old Slow Trot." Little did they or Old Slow Trot suspect that he was training most of them for active service as Union and Confederate cavalry officers in the coming War Between the States.

Thomas was 36 years old then, and still a bachelor. At the time, a frequent visitor at West Point was the widow of a prosperous hardware merchant whose nephew was a member of the Class of 1852. Thomas began to court one of her daughters, Frances Lucretia Kellogg. The couple did not dally with the romance. Within months they were married, at the home of the bride's uncle in Troy, New York.

While on his honeymoon, Thomas received a captain's commission. Nearly 10 years since he had been made a first lieutenant, the promotion was considered long overdue. Less than six months later, however, Thomas was uprooted from domestic life. In May of 1854 he was named commander of Company A, Third Artillery, and was ordered to Fort Yuma, in the Arizona Territory, near the California border.

The assignment was far from the domestic tranquility of West Point. The route to the desolate post out west required a boat trip to the Isthmus of Panama, an overland march of some 50 miles to the Pacific Ocean, and another sea voyage north to San Francisco, which he accomplished within 30 days. At Fort Yuma, his days grew long and lonely. It was a relatively satisfying post, nevertheless, and gratified his more than casual interest in nature. Thomas collected some plant and mineral specimens and a previously unknown variety of bat, a stuffed specimen of which still sits in the Smithsonian Institution in Washington, D.C.

Within a year, Thomas was chosen for a cavalry regiment that was organized to patrol the expanding western frontier. Unusual care had been taken in the selection of officers. Jefferson Davis, a fellow Virginian, was secretary of war, and his choice of Thomas was dictated not merely by Thomas's ability, but also by state loyalties. Captain Thomas was appointed junior major in the Second Cavalry and joined his new regiment in Missouri, at Jefferson Barracks.

The following spring the regiment was ordered to Camp Cooper, 170 miles north of Brownsville, Texas, where a strong hand was needed to search out Kiowa and Comanche Indians who had strayed from their reservations. One morning his troops had a close encounter with a party of 11 mounted Comanches. The Indians had stolen some small animals from one of the nearby settlements, then fled into a deep ravine. Thomas and his men followed, and arrows began to fly from the escaping Indians. One of these shafts glanced off his chin and lodged in his chest. By himself Thomas pulled the arrow from his chest and galloped back to Camp Cooper to dress his wound.

It was there, in the obscurity of garrison life in Texas, that Thomas watched from a distance the gradual approach of the inevitable conflict between North and South. He still considered himself a proud Virginian, but he never for a moment doubted where his duty lay.

Early in November 1860, he left Texas on a long leave of absence. Still in the East at the outbreak of the Civil War, he was ordered to return to Texas and take charge of his regiment. Thomas's commander there, General Robert E. Lee, had already tendered his resignation from the United States Army to enter the Confederate forces.

Obeying orders, Thomas brought his regiment to Carlisle, Pennsylvania. On the way he heard of the Confederate bombardment of Fort Sumter, the opening artillery round of the Civil War. Unmoved by the jubilation in the South over the incident, he renewed his oath to the United States upon reaching Carlisle. He never flinched from his allegiance to the Union, even when his home state of Virginia seceded.

Thomas accepted an appointment as colonel of the Fifth U.S. Cavalry. At the head of a brigade in General Patterson's army, he soon crossed the Potomac into Virginia and put to flight an insurgent militia of his own state. In August, he was appointed a brigadier general of volunteers and reported to the Army of the Cumberland three weeks later. At Camp Dick Robinson, 100 miles south of Cincinnati, the volunteers had responsibility for protecting all of Kentucky and Tennessee.

Thomas found the whole of Kentucky in turmoil. The camp itself was swarming with unorganized Kentucky regiments and crowds of refugees from east Tennessee, all of them eager to be armed and led back to drive the Confederate sympathizers from their homes.

General Thomas devoted himself to full-time instruction of the new recruits. It required great patience to impose on these independent backwoodsmen any semblance of military discipline. But soon they came to respect their general. They spoke of him as "Pap" Thomas and felt the sort of confidence in him that children might feel in a father.

Thomas, however, could be fastidious to the point of exasperation. He is said to have remarked to a less tidy officer, "The fate of an army may depend on a buckle." At the same time, his men trusted him implicitly. His whole nature and disposition was orderly, gentle, and kind. In fact, he abhorred war, not merely because of its cruelty, but also because of the chaos it caused.

Thomas soon sent the 1st Brigade of the Army of the Cumberland 30 miles southeast to resist a group of rebels who had entered Kentucky through the Cumberland Gap. Hoping to move the Kentuckians into east Tennessee, he set out on a 19-day march. The roads were almost impassable all the way to Logan's Crossroads. There, in the Cumberland Gap, he found himself cut off from the rest of the army.

About to be chewed up, Thomas stood, grim and defiant, the tall mountain walls protecting his forces from another Confederate assault. Three times he fell back into the protection of the gap. At last the whole force of the rebel army poured in. Near total exhaustion after two days of hard fighting, without food, rest or any reinforcements, Thomas showed not a hint of despair. He rallied, and what was left of his shattered force gave one last push.

A frightful slaughter followed on both sides, but once General Zollicoffer, leader of the Confederate assault, was killed, his troops were driven in confusion from the field. During the night that followed, most of the Confederate army escaped across the river, leaving guns, small arms and other spoils. Many of the wealthy rebels in middle Tennessee were so terrified by this defeat that they fled, with slaves and property, to Alabama and Mississippi.

Before Mill Springs, as the battle was known, Thomas was regarded as a competent officer. Now he was considered a general who could hold any terrain against overwhelming odds. Mill Springs was also the first real victory for the Union since its embarrassing disaster at Bull Run. The war was still young, and the North had badly needed a victory to boost its morale. Thomas had delivered.

In the spring Thomas was promoted to major general and offered the job of his commander, General Don Carlos Buell, who had caused great dissatisfaction in Washington. It was a chance for military glory, but Thomas declined. In his answer to Washington, he simply stated that Buell had already issued orders for a spring offensive. In October, nevertheless, a replacement was sent.

Although Thomas had declined to supercede Buell himself, he was outraged at the appointment of General William S. Rosecrans. Thomas tried to protest against serving under an officer who had been his junior. However, he acquiesced and served loyally after President Lincoln himself confirmed Rosecrans's commission.

Thomas's forces formed the central core of the Army of the Cumberland, when Confederate General Braxton Bragg, who Thomas had served with in Mexico, audaciously led his army from Chattanooga to the Ohio River. On the eve of 1863, Rosecrans met Bragg in bloody conflict on the banks of the Stones River. Succumbing to a huge charge of Bragg's forces at dawn, the whole right wing of the Union army was swept back three miles. The very existence of the Army of the Cumberland was imperiled.

But the center, under Thomas, held its ground and attacked the next day. Stubborn fighting by Thomas was the only thing that averted disaster. Rifle butts and bayonets were used against waves of Confederates rushing out of the trees toward the Union line.

After three days of fighting, the Confederates retreated into the night, surrendering Murfreesboro to seek safety in Chattanooga.

The Union army lay almost motionless until June when Rosecrans and Thomas met little resistance in driving Bragg out of Chattanooga. By now promoted to brigadier general, in Chattanooga Thomas found the affairs of the army in critical condition. Confederates had captured supply trains and destroyed a stretch of the Nashville and Chattanooga railroad. The only supply route included 60 miles of one of the worst mountain roads in the United States. Thomas placed his army on half-rations. Cavalry horses died by the scores daily.

While Thomas was being starved out of his stronghold in Chattanooga, the rebel forces were growing stronger by the day. They looked down on Thomas and his beleaguered forces from the heights of Lookout Mountain and Missionary Ridge, threatening to bombard the city. When a telegram from Grant directed Thomas to hold Chattanooga "at all hazards," Thomas replied, "We will hold the town till we starve."

Pap's men, to use their own language, were on "half rations of hard bread and beef dried on the hoof." He did all in his power to improve things. He strengthened defenses by having pontoons built and guns mounted around the city, then sent cavalry in search of forage. The picture brightened with the coming of reinforcements from the Army of the Potomac.

Measures were taken for the relief of Chattanooga. From every quarter troops were hurried, both to open communications and to reinforce the army. But the price of keeping Chattanooga would be high. Early in September, Bragg put forth titanic efforts to overwhelm the Union forces and win back the city.

Bragg camped his rebels on Chickamauga Creek, where he started hammering away at the Union army. Toward noon, a gap opened in Pap's right flank. His troops were bent back. Everyone south of him was driven in chaos back to Chattanooga. Only Thomas stood his ground. Now in command, he was still in the field with over half the army. Bragg was closing in on him, flushed with the hope of taking him as easy prey. The Union line was bent into a horseshoe shape, but not broken. From noon till night the battle raged. Every vicious assault upon the Union army was repelled. Thomas then launched the final assault of the day. When darkness brought an end to the bloody fighting, his lines were still intact, earning him the legendary nickname "the Rock of Chickamauga."

In the night, Thomas fell back. All the next day he waited for the expected attack, but the enemy was in no condition to mount it. The next day the whole Union army was safely back in Chattanooga. For the only time in its history, the Army of the Cumberland had left the enemy to bury its dead. The victory gave the Confederacy renewed hope after the major defeats it had suffered at Gettysburg and Vicksburg. But Thomas had inflicted such heavy losses that Bragg's ranks were badly depleted for the upcoming battle for Chattanooga.

There the Union army was besieged by Bragg's Confederates. With Grant commanding the army, plans were soon in the works for lifting the siege and attacking the Confederates, who still held fortified positions along the crests of Missionary Ridge and Lookout Mountain. In November, Thomas moved out from his defenses around the city and drove a light Confederate force from Orchard Knob, a low hill about a mile from the foot of Missionary Ridge. Union General William Tecumseh Sherman then attacked

The storming of Missionary Ridge
(Library of Congress)

and stormed the northern end of Missionary Ridge, but was repeatedly driven back.

Grant ordered Thomas to advance. Four of his divisions charged the ridge. Released from their long confinement in Chattanooga, Pap's jubilant bluecoats stormed the foot of the ridge and pursued the retreating rebels uphill, crowding so close upon them that the rebels on the crest hesitated to shoot downward for fear of hitting their own men. In an overwhelming charge, they took the summit and swept over it. Missionary Ridge still lives in history as one of the most extraordinary and daring assaults ever attempted.

With Bragg's retreat, most of Tennessee, containing many important rail centers and food-producing regions, was now in Union hands. And Grant was elevated to the position of commander of all U.S. armies. Without hesitation he put his old friend General William Tecumseh Sherman in charge of the entire western theater of war. Again Thomas was made subordinate to an officer who was his junior in years and rank; a year earlier, in fact, Sherman had been a division commander under him.

Many generals under similar circumstances would have asked to be relieved of their commands. But Thomas knew and respected Sherman's abilities. If he took umbrage, he didn't show it at the time. Perhaps he had learned something from his earlier dispute with Lincoln and Rosecrans.

When Thomas set out with Sherman for Atlanta in May of 1864, he brought with him 65,000 hardened veterans of his Army of the Cumberland. The march was an extraordinary hardship for 100 days. Thomas was constantly engaged in scores of battles along the way, and his forces were the first to enter Atlanta upon its surrender.

It was now suggested that his army be detached from Sherman's command and sent on a march to the sea. But after the defeat of Atlanta, Confederate General John Bell Hood had rallied his beaten and shattered forces. It was decided that Sherman's main force should make its now famous march to Atlanta; Thomas was ordered to stop any mischief by Hood.

While Sherman's army set out on its famous march through Georgia, Thomas enticed Hood westward, to fight him—if he would fight—in the neighborhood of Nashville. The plan worked perfectly. Lacking a leg and the use of one arm, Hood had to be strapped to the saddle each morning, but he fought as fiercely and as recklessly as possible. He followed the course of the Tennessee River, while Thomas fell back slowly but steadily in front of him.

Hood's Army of the Tennessee moved forward, confident of an easy victory. Soon the entire force that had confronted Sherman on his way to Atlanta was threatening Thomas. But Pap kept pace, retreating and delaying Hood as he went, and collecting reinforcements of new troops from Mississippi and Virginia.

Grant urged an attack by Thomas. But Thomas insisted that he was not yet strong enough to gain a decisive victory. The task thrust upon him seemed almost overwhelming. It was midwinter and Thomas had moved 200 miles from his main base of supplies. Worse still, nearly all of his mounted force had joined Sherman in the march to Savannah.

Grant grew impatient over what he considered a needless delay. Finally, on December 9, he issued an order relieving Thomas of command. Pap's fitness for independent command, and even his loyalty, were seriously in question. Soon the question was made irrelevant. Thomas reported himself ready to move, and the order was suspended.

A terrible storm of sleet and rain, freezing as it fell, caused yet another delay. Grant, now pursuing Lee in the eastern theater, dispatched another general with orders to replace Thomas. Before he arrived, however, a thaw began. After waiting for Hood to launch a frontal attack at Franklin, Thomas's line exploded with rifle and cannon fire, driving the rebels back beyond the Duck River.

Thomas had lured Hood into a doomed frontal attack that cost the Confederate commander an irreplaceable 6,200 casualties. Pap's confident troops, who had never lost faith in their leader, dealt so severe a blow that they wrecked Hood's army. The loss of 12 Confederate generals decimated the command of the Army of Tennessee. Thomas followed up and attacked the feeble remnant of Hood's army in Nashville. Hood bolted south toward the Tennessee River, and Thomas stayed right on his heels, taking prisoners and supplies at every swoop.

The weary and discouraged rebels came together some weeks later in Mississippi, nearly 250 miles from Thomas. In their haste to get away, they had thrown everything aside. Rifles, blankets, knapsacks, everything was abandoned. Thomas had utterly ruined the proud Army of Tennessee, which had advanced so boldly into Union-occupied territory. As an army, it never again took the field.

The battle of Nashville was substantially the end of the rebellion in Tennessee. For victory in that battle, Thomas received the appointment of major general in the U.S. Army, accompanied by the assurance of the secretary of war that "no commander has more justly earned promotion by devoted, disinterested and valuable services to his country."

Thomas was about to send his troops into winter quarters when Grant asked him to help organize a cavalry group to round up rebel remnants in the South. With a force of about 15,000, the cavalry pounded through Selma and Montgomery, Alabama, and captured the fugitive Confederate president, Jefferson Davis.

Thomas remained in command of this region for some years after. With the close of the war, he bent all his energies to the restoration of peace and order throughout the region. In 1868, President Johnson sent Thomas's name to the Senate for promotion to the brevet ranks of lieutenant general and general. Believing that the purpose of these promotions was to use him as an instrument for displacing General Grant as commander of the army, Thomas declined.

In that same year he was strongly urged to become a candidate for the presidency, but he refused to allow his name to be used. In June 1869, he assumed command of the Military Division of the Pacific, at San Francisco. There he died of apoplexy the following spring, leaving a widow but no children.

George Henry Thomas deserves to be ranked among the greatest generals of the U.S. Civil War. Of all the military questions arising from the conflict, one of the most fascinating is how Thomas took so many shots and kept coming. His steadiness and self-confidence under fire was outstanding. He was a general who simply could not be driven from ground he was given to hold.

Thomas always insisted on establishing fixed bases of supply and making lines of communication sure before advancing very far into enemy country. It is true that many other commanders who had learned how to cut loose from their defenses could move faster and farther in the field than Thomas. But while his deliberateness was often looked upon as sluggishness, Thomas never lost a battle.

Says Civil War scholar Bruce Catton, "Thomas comes down in history as the Rock of Chickamauga, the great defensive fighter, the man who could never be driven away, but who was not much on the offensive. That may be a correct appraisal. Yet it may also be worth making note that just twice in all the war was a major Confederate army driven away from a prepared position in complete rout—at Chattanooga and at Nashville. Each time the blow that routed it was launched by Thomas."

Chronology

July 31, 1816	born in Newsom's Depot, Virginia
July 1840	graduates West Point
1840	commissioned 2nd lieutenant
1844	promoted to 1st lieutenant
1851	instructor at West Point
November 17, 1852	marries Frances Lucretia Kellogg
1854	joins 2nd Cavalry, Jefferson Barracks
April 14, 1861	joins Union at Carlisle, Penn.
August 17, 1861	brigadier general of volunteers
January 19, 1862	wins battle of Mill Springs
April 25, 1862	made major general of volunteers
December 31, 1862	battle of Stones River
September 19, 1863	battle of Chickamauga
October 27, 1863	made brigadier general
November 1863	seized Missionary Ridge
November 30, 1864	battle of Franklin
December 15–16, 1864	battle of Nashville
March 3, 1865	made major general in Regular Army
June 1869	commands Military Division of the Pacific
March 28, 1870	dies in San Francisco

Further Reading

Cleaves, Freeman. *Rock of Chickamauga*. Westport, Conn.: Greenwood Press, 1974. A well-written biography of Thomas, including his personal life, with a focus on his military achievements.

Juergensen, Hans. *Major General George Henry Thomas*. Tampa: American Studies Press, 1980. An interesting summary of the life of Thomas.

Palumbo, Frank A. *George Henry Thomas: Major General, U.S.A.* Dayton: Morningside House, 1983. A good look at Thomas as a general, his tactics and strategies.

William Tecumseh Sherman
Scourge of the South

William Tecumseh Sherman
(Library of Congress)

"**W**ar is all hell," William Tecumseh Sherman said, and he aimed to bring that hell to the Confederacy. Sherman saw from the beginning how hard on everyone war was going to be. When he made his statement, he was retired from the army and under suspicion of insanity. Soon he was reinstated, brought back to crush half the Confederacy with destructive marches that shocked the civilized world. Sherman, it seemed, wasn't so crazy after all. In some ways, he was the first truly modern general. He was the first, in American history at least, to understand that civilians were the backbone of war. To break the back of the Confederacy, he made war directly against its civilians.

Tecumseh Sherman, named by his father in honor of a great Indian chief, was born in Lancaster, Ohio, on February 8, 1820. The family was originally from New England, and had come to America from England in the 17th century. Two hundred years later, his mother and father, who was a lawyer and in his later years a justice of the Ohio Supreme Court, migrated to what was then the unsettled West and made their home in Ohio. They married and had 11 children, of whom William was the sixth.

When "Cump," as William was called, was only nine, his father died, leaving his mother a large family of children without adequate financial support. Sherman and his younger brother John were farmed out to a family friend, Thomas Ewing, who would one day be a U.S. senator and serve in the Cabinets of three presidents.

When the Ewings learned that Cump had not been baptized, he was given the name William Tecumseh Sherman, perhaps because the Catholic priest objected to an Indian name without a Christian first name to precede it. At Ewing's home the boys were surrounded by talkative and energetic farmers, lawyers and politicians. While brother John would later become a politician and serve as U.S. senator from Ohio, William enrolled at West Point.

Tall and red-haired, intelligent and a bit irritable, William was an outspoken cadet even though he was only 16 when he entered the academy. A bit odd, too, he slept little, talked a lot, and was always boiling over with ideas. He wore shoes rather than military boots, and was rumpled in dress. Sherman himself admitted that he was not considered a good soldier, but he was at least a good student. He graduated 6th in his class of 42, the survivors of 141 cadets who had entered the military academy four years before.

At the time he expressed a desire to go west, far away from civilization, to the new frontiers that were opening up. But after graduation in 1840, he was assigned to the Third Artillery and served for six years in the South. First he was based in Florida, where the embers of the Seminole Wars were still smoldering. In

1842, he was sent to Fort Morgan, in Alabama, and later that year he was transferred to South Carolina, at Fort Moultrie.

The immediate vicinity of the fort served as a summer resort for the people of Charleston, and life at Fort Moultrie acquainted him with many of the political and social leaders of the South. Sherman's personality shined in the high-spirited atmosphere of Southern hunting society. At this time, and in fact up to the outbreak of the Civil War, Sherman was probably better acquainted with Southern life and manners than with Northern ways. In 1843, on his return from a short leave, he began to study law. Sherman said he took up law not to make it his profession, but to render himself a more intelligent soldier.

When the Mexican War began in 1846 he was sent with troops around Cape Horn to California. As an adjutant general, Sherman was busy for four years trying to incorporate the occupied Mexican province as a territory of the United States government. His legal background was a great asset to him, even though he had never actually begun the practice of law. In temperament as well he was suited to the task, revealing all the sternness and determination of a man bent on untangling the logistical problems of the American occupation.

In 1850, he left San Francisco, returned to Ohio, and married Senator Ewing's daughter, Ellen Boyle Ewing. Her father, Sherman's old friend, was then secretary of the interior. Sherman was made a captain in the Commissary Department and served for a short time in St. Louis and New Orleans.

Seeing little prospect for promotion and small opportunity for his talents in the army during peacetime, Sherman realized there was plenty of demand for West Point graduates in civilian life. In 1853 he resigned so that he might return to California to take charge of a banking establishment, the San Francisco branch of Lucas, Turner and Co., of St. Louis.

Returning again to San Francisco, Sherman was cautious and successful as a banker. Soon his was considered one of the best banks on the Pacific coast. Through prudent management he was able to weather the storm that destroyed nearly all the California banks in 1856 and 1857. Nevertheless, Sherman had been reporting to his headquarters in St. Louis that the bank could not continue to make profits under the existing conditions. In 1857 his advice was accepted, and the business closed.

Sherman then accepted the appointment of general of militia in order to put down the Vigilantes. This was a loose group of self-appointed law enforcers formed in San Francisco to crush the lawlessness that had arisen as a natural result of the weakness and corruption of the local government.

Sherman sympathized with the desire of the local citizens to put down disorder. The tens of thousands of newcomers who had come to California as goldseekers included numerous criminals. Most were unmarried men, in haste to get rich. Reckless speculation, loose living, and extravagance were common in many places.

Sherman maintained that the proper authorities should be called upon to assume their responsibilities, and that illegal methods of repressing crime should not be tolerated. He was only partially successful; the support promised him by the U.S. military authorities never materialized. And the citizens continued to dislike and distrust the local authorities.

In 1858 he went to Kansas, where he was admitted to the bar and finally started to practice law. With his brother-in-law, he formed the firm of Ewing, Sherman and McCook. Sherman's career was insignificant and rather humorous. He lost his only legal case, a dispute over the possession of a shanty, but joined with his client to defeat the judgment by destroying the house at night!

Sherman had shown he lacked the temperament for settling disputes in the courtroom. He quit the practice of law and undertook army contracts for constructing military roads. Sherman opened a large tract of Kansas land for Senator Ewing. Bored and fed up with business life, however, Sherman eventually decided to reenter the army. He applied for paymastership, but his friends in the War Department recommended him instead for the superintendency of the Louisiana State Seminary. Now known as Louisiana State University, it was being organized when Sherman was chosen as superintendent in 1859. For the third time in his life, Sherman made his home in the South.

He was an efficient college executive. The seminary was soon organized and running like clockwork. Students and instructors alike were under Sherman's careful direction. He soon became a favorite, not only with "his boys" but also with the faculty of young professors. He had no classes, but gave occasional instruction in American history and geography, and on Fridays conducted the "speaking." He was a good storyteller, and frequently his room would be crowded with students and young professors, all listening to his descriptions of army life and of the great, wild West.

Due, perhaps, to his long experience in the West, Sherman regarded slavery as the cause of the sectional troubles of 1860 and 1861. It was all the result, he maintained, of the machinations of unscrupulous politicians scheming for power. When Louisiana seceded, he announced publicly what was already generally known, that he would not remain at the seminary. He could take no part against the United States. It was said that he had wept bitterly on hearing of the secession of South Carolina.

One of the strongest arguments against secession was, in his opinion, the geographic one. Familiar with all the Southern country, especially the Mississippi Valley, he insisted that the South ought to struggle within the Union for a redress of grievances. He believed that the South, though itself at fault, was justifiably aggrieved. But he could not be prevailed upon to remain. In February 1861, he resigned and headed North.

Sherman at once went to Washington where he found the politicians busy. As they and Lincoln were "too radical" to suit him, he left. "You politicians," he told his brother, "have got things in a hell of a fix, and you may get them out as best you can. I will have nothing more to do with it."

For two months he was president of a street-railway company in St. Louis. While there he witnessed the division of Missouri into hostile and opposing camps. He watched as the North gradually make up its mind to fight. When Fort Sumter fell, he put his uniform back on and reluctantly went to war.

Of the duration of the war he took what was then considered an extreme view. "You might as well attempt to put out the flames of a burning house with a squirt gun," he said. "I think this is to be a long war, very long, much longer than any politician thinks."

Sherman regarded President Lincoln's call for 75,000 men for three months of service as trifling with a serious matter. He declared that the uprising of the secessionists was not a mob riot to be put down by unruly vigilantes, but a war to be fought out by armies.

Sherman offered his service to the War Department and was appointed colonel of the 13th United States Infantry. He saw his first action at Manassas, or Bull Run, where he commanded a brigade of four regiments. Although it was routed, he quickly restored its organization and morale. For this he was made a brigadier general of volunteers.

Transferred to Kentucky to assist General Robert Anderson, his former commander, in organizing the Federals of that border state, Sherman soon found himself in command when Anderson took ill. Few people were prepared for the curious problem of Kentucky politics. Upon the outbreak of the Civil War, Kentucky had attempted to maintain a position of neutrality, but the geographic position of the state made the plan impossible. It was expected that Kentuckians could be persuaded to keep their state in the Union, but the governor had rejected President Abraham Lincoln's appeal for troops. When Confederate and Union armies began to pour into the state from opposite directions, formal demands were actually made by Kentucky for their withdrawal.

When the Union armies took up position, Washington expected that the number of men required would be few. But Sherman soon disabused the army of this notion. He declared that 60,000 men would be needed to drive the enemy out of the state and 200,000 to put an end to the struggle in that region. Most people considered his prescience as craziness. Insisting that he was better acquainted with the Southern temper than were the Northern politicians and the newspapers, Sherman almost ruined his career with the frankness of his speech to the secretary of war and to newspaper men.

For such statements some journalists thought he'd gone mad. Newspapers declared him insane, and noted dourly that an air of hysteria seemed to characterize all of his actions. Reporters hounded him for several months and almost drove him from his command. This only fed Sherman's contempt for the lot of them. He considered reporters worse than spies because he felt they printed military secrets just to sell newspapers.

"These dirty newspaper scribblers have the impudence of Satan," he complained. "They come into camp, poke about like lazy sharks and pick up their camp rumors and publish them as facts. They're a pest, and I treat them as spies, which in truth they are." Sherman said he was convinced that if he killed them all, "there would be news from hell before breakfast."

Sherman continued to insist that at least 200,000 men would be needed to suppress the rebellion in the Western theater of the war. No one believed him. He grew melancholy, prone to fits of anxiety and rage, and many now thought he was plainly insane. In November of 1861, Sherman was relieved as Union commander in Kentucky. December found him at home in the care of his wife. He'd gone home saying he would kill himself were it not for the disgrace it would bring on his children.

During the next year Sherman shook off the melancholy that had sent him home in December. His brother, the United States senator, helped arrange for Sherman to be restored to his division. Sherman put his checkered career behind him and reported to General Halleck, commanding the Department of the West.

A movement had begun to control the Mississippi Valley, the key to the West. From the beginning of the war this had been one of Sherman's favorite strategies: Seize control of the Mississippi and cut the Confederacy in two. Now there was a growing feeling that the river must be opened, and the Mississippi Valley must belong to one people.

At that time General Ulysses S. Grant was in command of a force in Tennessee that was moving on Fort Henry and Fort Donelson. Just after the capture of these strongholds, Sherman was assigned to command an Ohio division in the Army of the Tennessee. Sherman's men were encamped on the uplands between Pittsburgh Landing and a log-built Methodist church called Shiloh. Early on the morning of April 6, Confederate commander Albert Sidney Johnston launched a surprise attack.

Sherman's divisions were overrun by the initial attack. The air was filled with panic. Sherman himself was wounded in the hand, taking two bullet wounds as he desperately tried to hold the lines. Bleeding badly, he did not leave the field. He stuck to his guns and held out long enough for Grant to form a new line on a ridge overlooking the Tennessee River.

The next morning, after General Don Carlos Buell had joined them during the night, Grant ordered Sherman to advance with the combined Union armies of the Tennessee and the Ohio. Steadily they pushed back the Confederate Army of Mississippi, which withdrew to Corinth. The Union did not pursue, but the Confederate enemy left Corinth by late May.

Shiloh, after Grant's victories at Fort Henry and Fort Donelson, marked another step toward cutting the Confederacy in half. The railroad from Memphis to Chattanooga was severed. This left only the forts near Vicksburg on the Mississippi River in Southern hands.

But the "victory" at Shiloh had also resulted in more deaths than all other American wars combined. Shiloh had taught the North what Sherman had been saying all along, that the country had a very bloody affair on its hands. Now he was no longer regarded as insane. Instead he was considered one of the best of the minor generals, and was made a major general of volunteers for his services in the Shiloh-Corinth campaign.

Grant then ordered Sherman to Memphis, with instructions to control its rebellious inhabitants. Sherman clamped down on Memphis like a vise. He quickly suppressed guerrilla warfare, directed all who adhered to the Confederate cause to leave the city, forbade the citizens to trade in cotton, would not permit the use of Confederate money, and allowed no freed slaves to be returned by force to their masters.

The next step was to capture Vicksburg and thereby open the Mississippi River to Union navigation. The river city was strongly fortified and was covered by an army commanded by General Pemberton, posted behind the Tallahatchie River. The first attempt to capture the Confederate stronghold called for a two-pronged attack.

Grant detached Sherman, escorted by a Union gunboat fleet via water, to capture Vicksburg while he, Grant, held Pemberton. Sherman's expeditionary force boarded transports at Memphis, then headed down the Mississippi, and up the Yazoo River, just north of Vicksburg. While Grant preoccupied Confederate troops in northern Mississippi, Sherman's troops disembarked and were supposed to take control of the bluffs that were a gateway to the city just to their south.

Sherman was on his own, however, after Grant was forced to withdraw, his supply base having been destroyed by raiding Confederate cavalry. Days later, after shelling the Confederate forces, part of Sherman's expeditionary force found five narrow approaches to the bluffs. All these were well covered by Confederate infantry and artillery. Sherman nevertheless ordered nine regiments to charge through lakes and bayous toward the foot of the Walnut Hills.

Exposed to fire, the helpless Northerners were easily picked off as they forged their way over the marshland. Yet Sherman would not relent. He ordered his men to rush the center of the Confederate defenses overlooking the Chickasaw Bayou. They did, and were met by a storm of shells, canisters and minié balls. Sherman's attack was firmly repulsed. On January 2, 1863, he finally withdrew from the Yazoo River.

The next spring Sherman returned to Vicksburg with Grant. Sherman moved first, taking the hills overlooking the Yazoo River, possession of which assured Grant's reinforcement and supply from the North. The Union Army of the Tennessee now faced a very strong line of trenches and forts surrounding the

Confederate city. Inside these works were General Pemberton and 32,000 Confederate soldiers.

Grant wasted no time, deciding to attack before Pemberton had time to post his defenses strongly. Sherman was the only other Union commander prepared for an attack. His troops made it as far as the walls of the Confederate fort but, unable to force a breakthrough, were repulsed, losing 1,000 men.

By May 25, Grant and Sherman realized they couldn't take Vicksburg by storm, and they began siege operations. The city was shelled around the clock by Union army and naval batteries. Sickness and hunger finally forced the Confederates to surrender. On July 4, the Union entered Vicksburg.

It was through the eventual success of the Vicksburg campaign in 1863, which effectively cut the Confederacy in two, that both Sherman and Grant secured their reputations. Henceforth generals who were political appointees were less in evidence, and the professional soldier came to the fore. Grant was called upon to exercise the chief command of all the armies of the Union. Sherman was made a brigadier general of regulars and was given supervision of the entire Southwest.

Vicksburg also cemented his friendship with General Grant. Grant enjoyed Sherman's rapid-fire brilliance and was grateful for the dispatch with which he carried out every order. Sherman admired his friend's cool temper, his steadiness in the midst of crisis, and what he called Grant's simple faith in success. They trusted each other implicitly.

Sherman was now to command the chief army that was to strike at the vitals of the lower South. An army of 100,000 men under his direction was to hold the Mississippi Valley in Tennessee, which contained many important rail centers and food-producing regions. Ordered to march to Chattanooga, he lost no time in doing so, repairing roads as he went.

At the north end of Missionary Ridge, after crossing Chickamauga Creek, Sherman resisted fierce assaults delivered in sudden succession. It was clear that the enemy was doing everything it could to crush him. But Sherman was elusive, drawing his foe to his flank while the main Union army captured the ridge. Sherman attacked and seized the north end of Missionary Ridge, only to find that a wide, deep ravine separated him from the main Confederate works. The next day he pushed south, repeatedly attacked the heavily fortified Confederate right, and held on until the rest of the Union Army of the Cumberland stormed the ridge.

Sherman would now set out through the mountains of northern Georgia for Atlanta. His invasion of Georgia was part of Grant's grand Union strategy—to seize Atlanta, an industrial hub of the South, and smash the combined Confederate forces of Bragg's Army of Tennessee and General Johnston's Army of Mississippi.

For three months in Georgia, Sherman was pitted against General Joseph E. Johnston. Outgunned, outsupplied, and outnumbered almost two to one, Johnston could hope only to slow Sherman's three armies or lure them into a frontal attack. The advance was a masterpiece of planning. In a matter of hours,

General Sherman marches his army into Georgia.
(National Archives)

Sherman's engineers would replace burned bridges and repair ripped-up rail lines. Through May and June of 1864 he steadily advanced toward Atlanta. Slowly, relentlessly, he forced Johnston, with his smaller force, out of each entrenchment.

In late June at Kennesaw Mountain, just north of Atlanta, the Confederates dug in. Tired of flanking movements, Sherman tried a frontal assault. His Union soldiers stormed up the mountain and were hurled back. Sherman lost 3,000 men, Johnston only 750. One or two more such assaults, an aide told Sherman, would use up his army. Sherman called off the attack. He never admitted he had made a mistake at Kennesaw Mountain, but he never repeated it either. The Confederates had handed Sherman his worst defeat. They also delayed his advance on Atlanta for a few days, but in the end Sherman's superior numbers made up for this defeat.

Reluctantly, Sherman returned to his slow flanking maneuvers, forcing Johnston back until he was within sight of Atlanta itself. There Sherman stalled. Two months of relentless fighting had resulted in a stalemate. North of Atlanta, he would have to blast through a seemingly impenetrable system of trenches and fortifications to take the city. Everyone knew Atlanta was the key to winning the war. Sherman's goal was to sever the railroads supplying Atlanta. If he were to isolate the railroad hub of the South, the war could be brought to a quick conclusion.

When the Union army finally reached the outskirts of Atlanta, the Confederate commander was replaced by 33-year-old John B. Hood of Texas. Sherman was delighted with Hood, sure he would be attacked by the impetuous young Southern general. Such an attack would be doomed. Many of Sherman's units were now armed with Henry repeating rifles, capable of firing 15 shots without being reloaded. Outgunned rebels complained the Yankees could now reload on a Sunday and keep shooting all week.

As expected, Hood rushed to protect his supply lines. The battle of Atlanta had begun in earnest. In less than 30 minutes, Hood was forced to withdraw. West of the city, Hood again tried to rout Sherman's army. Again, he failed. A third of Hood's army was gone, 22,000 men killed and wounded, and Hood fell back into Atlanta.

Behind their ramparts, the Confederates waited for Sherman to attack, but Sherman saw no need to be so rash. He sealed off supplies from the Macon & Western railroad and began to shell the heavily fortified Confederate trenches and the city beyond.

Sherman's army marches south, leaving Atlanta in flames.
(Library of Congress)

Finally, on August 31 at Jonesborough, Hood struck the Union flank in an effort to protect his supply lines. Sherman hurled most of his army against the railroad, and broke Hood's grip. During the night, the Confederates pulled out. The next day Sherman marched in. "Atlanta is ours, and fairly won," said Sherman. For his success in this campaign, he was made a major general in the regular army.

With Hood in retreat from Atlanta, Sherman was now free to move eastward through the almost totally undefended country-side to the Atlantic seaboard. From Atlanta, in late 1864, he proposed to march his army through the heart of Georgia all the way to Savannah. His army would live off the land, destroying everything in its path that could conceivably aid the faltering Confederacy, and a good deal that couldn't.

Before leaving Atlanta, Sherman ordered all townspeople, white and black, out of their homes, then directed his men to burn or destroy anything that could be of help to the rebels. Local civilians looted the town and helped spread the blaze throughout the city. Then Sherman turned to the southeast and began his march. His army's supply train stretched behind him for 25 miles. Sixty-two thousand men moved forward in two great columns.

Sherman threatened Augusta and Macon, but found little to oppose him in his march to the sea. His army looted all the way, destroying what it could not carry and tearing up railroads. Sherman forbade his men to plunder the homes they passed, but neither he nor they took the order very seriously. "I've got a regiment that can kill, gut and scrape a pig without breaking ranks," he bragged.

The troops burned everything in their path. As far as the eye could see, flames lit up the sky. They looted slave cabins as well as mansions. Twenty-five thousand slaves nevertheless fled to Sherman's army, rejoicing that he had come to liberate them. At one Georgia town, Sherman's army lit bonfires of Confederate currency. They held a mock session of the legislature that passed a resolution returning the state to the Union. Before they were through, Sherman and his men would cross 425 miles of hostile territory, wreaking $100 million worth of havoc. The South would never forget.

Late in January of 1865 Sherman started north for the Carolinas with his artillery and supply wagons. A relentless winter rain was falling and Confederate generals were confident that no army could march through the mud. But Sherman and his men marched a steady 10 miles a day.

Now North and South Carolina lay helpless in his path. "My aim was to whip the rebels, to humble their pride and follow them to their innermost recesses, and to make them fear and dread us," Sherman said. "War is cruelty," he added. "There is no use trying to reform it. The crueler it is, the sooner it will be over."

Thus began the march north through the Carolinas, which was more difficult than the march to the sea. Battalions of ax-wielding infantrymen led the way, hacking down whole forests to construct corduroy roads with the logs. South Carolina suffered even more than Georgia, because it had been the first state to secede. Few houses were left standing. On February 17, 1865, the Confederates abandoned all of Charleston, along with Fort Sumter, where the first shots of the Civil War had been fired nearly four years earlier.

When General Robert E. Lee surrendered in Virginia, the Confederates in North Carolina gave up soon afterward. In a farmhouse near Durham Station, North Carolina, the bulk of the South's already decimated military might surrendered to Sherman. The war was practically over.

By late May, with the American flag flying at full staff above the White House for the first time since Lincoln's death, Ulysses S. Grant and the new president, Andrew Johnson, stood side by side to watch the grand armies pass in review down Pennsylvania Avenue from the U.S. Capitol. The great procession took two days.

The crowds cheered loudest the second day, as Sherman rode past at the head of his great army.

Sherman remained a soldier, fighting Indians and shunning politics until his retirement. "If nominated, I will not run," he told a Republican delegation urging him to run for president. "If elected, I will not serve."

When Grant was made president, Sherman succeeded him as general of the armies. Knowing that Grant's views coincided with his own, he hoped to reorganize the military so that the commanding general, not the secretary of war, would be the real commander-in-chief. With Grant's assistance the reforms were undertaken, but they lasted less than a month. The political pressure upon Grant to favor the old system was too strong for him to resist.

Sherman and Grant then drifted apart. Sherman could do little to carry out his plans for the improvement of the army. Finally, he moved his headquarters to St. Louis, where he remained until President Hayes invited him back to Washington. There he implemented his cherished reforms of army administration, until his retirement in 1884.

During his final years, Sherman spent most of his time in New York among old army associates. He attended reunions, made speeches at soldiers' celebrations, and put his papers in order for the use of future historians. He died in New York City in the winter of 1891, at age 71. He was buried, as he wished, in St. Louis.

Like other successful commanders in the Civil War, Sherman had attained the fullness of his powers only gradually. Not all military experts agree that he was a great commander on the battlefield. In his successful campaigns he was generally pitted against weaker forces. And he was aided by the blunders of his opponents.

But all agree that Sherman's temperament, his sternness and determination, made him eminently qualified to undertake the task of demolishing the weakened South. He was a great strategist if not so successful a tactician; he accomplished more by marching than by fighting. But he had a genius for estimating the capabilities of the enemy, and he was able to strike with irresistible force at the weak points in the defense.

One feature of Sherman's campaign, after leaving Atlanta, has been severely criticized. Much of the destruction of private property in Georgia and South Carolina, it is held, was not only unnecessary but also amounted to cruelty in depriving the population of the necessities of life. Sherman himself had said he would make Georgia "howl" and would "make its inhabitants feel that war and ruin are synonymous terms."

Bitter feelings on the subject still exist in the communities that Sherman marched over and plundered in 1864 and '65. But most Southern people have come to realize that, in the long run, Sherman's marches were a way of ending the war comparatively quickly, with little bloodshed. Of course, there were excesses. But the Southern people were still hopeful that their secession might yet succeed. The blow to Southern morale was far greater than the material destruction.

Sherman succeeded because he had "a concept of war and a determination to make it succeed," according to Civil War scholar James M. McPherson. "Like Lincoln, he believed in a hard war and a soft peace." Sherman, says McPherson, "recognized that only a thin line separated such plundering from the destruction of enemy resources and the morale necessary to win the war."

Chronology

February 8, 1820	born in Lancaster, Ohio
July 1, 1840	graduates West Point
November 30, 1841	first lieutenant
1846	adjutant general in California
May 1, 1850	marries Ellen Boyle Ewing
September 2, 1850	sent to St. Louis and New Orleans
September 6, 1853	resigns from army
1857	returns to St. Louis
1858	begins law practice in Kansas
May 13, 1861	made colonel in Union army
July 21, 1861	battle of Bull Run
August 3, 1861	made brigadier general
April 6–7, 1862	battle of Shiloh-Corinth
May 1, 1862	made major general of volunteers
September 1862	sent to Memphis
July 4, 1863	Vicksburg captured
November 26, 1863	captures Missionary Ridge
March 12, 1864	commands Army of the Mississippi
August 12, 1864	made major general in Regular Army
September 1, 1864	captures Atlanta
July 25, 1866	made lieutenant general
March 4, 1869	made general of U.S. Army
February 8, 1884	retires from army
February 14, 1891	dies in New York City

Further Reading

Barrett, John Gilchrist. *Sherman's March Through the Carolinas.* Chapel Hill: University of North Carolina Press, 1956. An examination of Sherman's often-overlooked, destructive march through the Carolinas.

Dodge, Granville Mellen. *Personal Recollections of President Abraham Lincoln, General Ulysses S. Grant, and General William T. Sherman.* Denver: Sage Books, 1965. A fascinating account of Sherman's influence on Grant and Lincoln.

Hart, Basil Henry Liddell. *Sherman: Soldier, Realist, American.* New York: Praeger, 1958. A detailed biography of Sherman, focusing on his personality and his love-hate relationship with the South.

Ulysses S. Grant
The Unlikely Conqueror

Ulysses S. Grant
(Library of Congress)

*U*lysses S. Grant, when he signed on with the Union army, had been a failure in almost everything in life except marriage. Already booted out of the army as a drunk, dumb luck put him back in uniform as a mustering officer when the war broke out between the Northern and Southern states. Three years later he was leading the Union army to victory. Four years after that, he was president of the United States.

President Abraham Lincoln picked Grant as the commander of the armies of the United States because he had faith in his willingness to fight. Six other generals had failed the North. Grant alone delivered. The man who had begun his wartime career with the faintest hope of distinguishing himself succeeded where others had failed because he understood so well the demands of war. He was quick to seize the initiative, persistent in pursuing enemies, and willing to take heavy casualties. His tenacity paid off when he crippled the army of the North's greatest foe, General Robert E. Lee.

At first a simple country lad, Hiram Ulysses Grant was born on April 27, 1822, in a little two-room cabin on the banks of the Ohio River, at Point Pleasant, Clermont County, Ohio. His grandfather, Captain Noah Grant, had been a Connecticut soldier in the Revolutionary Army, and in 1800 settled in Ohio.

His mother, Hannah Simpson, was of an American family of pioneers noted for their sturdy independence of character. She was a silent, religious woman with great common sense. It was from her that young 'Lyss, as she called him, inherited his steady temper. Like his mother, 'Lyss kept to himself, rarely uttering a word.

New sisters and brothers arrived with regularity, but 'Lyss was not particularly close to any of them. A quiet, harmless boy, he was unjustifiably considered a dullard. Acquaintances nicknamed him "Listless." Among close friends, however, he could be a lively talker, if the occasion served. Apparently, the reticence he inherited from his mother was tempered by an occasional lapse into the gregariousness of his father, Jesse Root Grant.

Jesse had established himself as a prosperous hide tanner in Ravenna, Illinois, before illness caused him to lose all he had gained in life. He soon moved the family to Point Pleasant, Ohio, a hamlet of a dozen houses on the Ohio River, five miles east of Cincinnati, and started all over, scraping cowhides for someone else. A year and a half after the birth of Ulysses, the family moved again, some 25 miles away to Georgetown, the seat of Brown County. Jesse had saved enough money to open a tannery of his own.

His business did well. He built a small brick home across a narrow alley from his tannery. Every day the odor of slaughtered animals wafted up to Ulysses's room. Young 'Lyss, who would someday preside over the slaughter of countless Confederates, was sickened by the smell and sight of bloody hides. He was an animal lover, so averse as a youth to inflicting pain that he abhorred the boyish sport of hunting.

Almost entirely self-taught, Jesse desired for his children the educational opportunities that had been denied him. From the time he was six years old until he was 17, 'Lyss regularly attended school. He was an indifferent student, however, average or below average in everything but math, which he excelled at.

There was one other area in which he showed much promise—he was a great hand with horses. His love of horses became a conspicuous passion. Soon men were paying him to break their young stock. Once, when a circus came to town, the ringmaster staked $5 on anyone who could sit on a wild pony. Under 'Lyss, the pony bolted and bucked. The ringmaster even tossed a monkey on 'Lyss's back. It climbed on his head and pawed at his face, but 'Lyss went home with the money.

Sometime thereafter 'Lyss was sent away to school for two winters. Jesse knew his son had no ambition but one, to get away from the dreadful tannery. If he had to, 'Lyss told his father, he would stay at the tannery until he was 21, but not a day longer. He said he would prefer to be a farmer or a river trader, or even become educated. Jesse figured he'd better get the boy an education.

While not a brilliant student, 'Lyss went on to win an appointment to the U.S. Military Academy at West Point. Another town boy with an appointment had dropped out, leaving a vacancy. Jesse wrote to one of his state senators and was given an audience with Ohio Congressman Thomas Hamer. An acceptance notice came, but it aroused no particular enthusiasm in 'Lyss. Nothing did.

When he registered at West Point, Ulysses transposed his given names, fearing that his initials, H.U.G., would make him an object of ridicule. At West Point he was told that his sponsoring congressman had reported his name as Ulysses Simpson Grant. Failing to obtain a correction from the authorities, he accepted the new designation uncomplainingly. Fellow cadets wondered what the "U.S." stood for. Some supposed it meant United States. Others said it was probably Uncle Sam. The Uncle Sam was shortened to Sam, and it stuck. From then on he was known as Sam Grant.

Although he was not a brilliant student according to the standards of West Point, Sam Grant made good use of the chance to train as a soldier. But for the most part he went unnoticed, leaving no significant impression on anyone, except with his horseback-riding abilities. As a rider he had no peer among the cadets. At the academic level, he graduated 21st in his class of 39.

When his orders for duty came down, they were decidedly unglamorous. As the best rider at West Point, he had requested a commission in the cavalry but was sent to the Fourth Infantry, Jefferson Barracks, St. Louis. He had already decided that upon serving one obligatory tour of duty he would resign his commission and become a math teacher. In the meantime, he figured, St. Louis might not be so bad. It was, for one thing, the home of his fourth-year West Point roommate, Frederick Tracy Dent.

Dent had a sister, Julia, and Lieutenant Grant found himself more and more drawn to the Dent home because of her. Whenever he could he would visit the Dent farm outside the city at White Haven. But after a brief courtship, he would see her only once again during the next four years. The Fourth Infantry had been ordered south to Louisiana to help man an observation post along the border with Mexico. Upon Grant's return four years later, he and Julia were married at White Haven.

In Corpus Christi, as part of what was termed the Army of Occupation in what is now Texas, Grant was not in sympathy with the Mexican War. To him the idea of conquest, justified to the Americans of the day as "Manifest Destiny," was plainly immoral. But as a second lieutenant he was in no position to challenge or to make policy. As regimental quartermaster, he joined the long march deep into the heart of Mexico.

For most of the war, Grant saw little action. As quartermaster, he was kept in the back with the mules and the wagon trains, packing kettles and mess kits and ammunition. But when the Army reached Monterrey, Grant went forward to see the artillery fire. Mounting his horse, he made a dash through the city to obtain ammunition for the troops.

In Mexico City he saw the Mexican batteries open up. American soldiers were dropping left and right outside the walls of the great fortress of Chapultepec. Grant showed he could think on his feet. He spotted a church belfry and realized it would command a broad view of the battle. Seizing an artillery piece, he and several others entered the church and carried the gun up to the belfry. From this perch Grant drove a crowd of Mexican defenders from the fortress gates, thus doing his part in the battle that led to U.S. victory in the war.

Grant emerged from the war as a first lieutenant and brevet captain, but no less averse to military life than he had always been. He and Julia soon found themselves at the post of Sacketts Harbor, New York, on the eastern shore of Lake Ontario. Grant found his work as a quartermaster unchallenging. In time orders came for him to go to the Pacific coast.

It was 1852, and the West was booming from the California gold rush. The route to the coast would be by ship to Panama, then across the narrow isthmus to the Pacific Ocean. No one could say with certainty how long the trip would take. There could be no question about taking Julia. The couple had one child already, and Julia was pregnant with the next. Grant seriously considered resigning from the army. Without another job offer, however, he hesitated.

The regiment arrived in Panama during the rainy season. The trip across the isthmus was a nightmare. Mules could not be obtained. Delays were incessant. Cholera broke out, and many died in the steamy, murderous heat. Grant, as quartermaster, buried the dead, encouraged the living, and put the sick in hammocks as they slowly made their way along thin trails blazed by Spaniards centuries before. When the decimated regiment reached the Pacific, the survivors took ship for the north, to Oregon. Those who lived through it remembered how cool and unrattled Grant had been in those days.

In Oregon, there was virtually nothing for Grant to do except keep an eye on Indians and wait for army surveying parties. Mail from the East took months to arrive. He often would sit for hours reading and rereading Julia's letters. One night he dreamt that she had given birth to a girl. At the time, Ulysses Grant Jr. was already five months old.

Grant was transferred south to Fort Humboldt in California, but life at this tiny frontier settlement was as dreary as it had been in Oregon. He had never been so sad and lonely before. At a local Indian trading store, he began to drink. It wasn't long before he developed a reputation as a drunkard. One warning from his commanding officer was breached, followed by a request for Grant's resignation. The year was 1854. Grant had spent 15 years in uniform. Now he was a civilian.

Out of the army, out of money, without a job, he drifted to San Francisco, then back to New York, and finally to Sacketts Harbor.

He was 32, with no money and no trade, married and with two children. The family decided to move to St. Louis. There, outside the city, his father-in-law had left a 60-acre farm to his daughter as a wedding present.

Grant tried farming and hauling wood, and even selling real estate in St. Louis. Nothing seemed to suit him. A man with an all-pervading air of bad luck, his acquaintances took to avoiding him on the streets. Christmas of 1859 found him pestering friends for loans. He was now 37, out of work, in debt, and miserably depressed.

At wit's end, Grant scratched up enough money for a train ticket to Galena, Illinois. There his father had set up his two other sons in a family leather-goods business. They agreed to take him in. Grant was happy that, at least, it was not the ghastly tannery. He settled down to a quiet routine, totalling bills by day and spending nights with his wife and children. For the first time in his life, Grant seemed content. But the quiet bliss of marriage and family life was soon shattered by the first shots of the Civil War.

When news of the bombardment of Fort Sumter reached Galena, the town went wild with militant fervor. There was, however, only one man there who had served in the Regular Army. His name was Grant, and he still wore his tattered old army bluecoat. "There are but two parties now, traitors and patriots, and I want hereafter to be ranked with the latter," Grant said.

He immediately pitched in, helping to train the mounting number of eager recruits. Once organized and taught the manual of arms, the volunteers he had trained went to the Illinois capital for induction into the state regiment. After they were sworn in, Grant marched behind his company, as a civilian. Still resigned from the army, he had not been re-instated to army service.

In Springfield, the choice positions of the regiment had already been handed out. Grant spent 10 days searching for work, then wrote home to his father that there was no room for him; he would not be staying long. By luck, Grant's pleas caught the ear of Governor Yates. Given a position as clerk in the adjutant general's office, Grant proved himself and was soon appointed colonel of an unruly volunteer regiment.

Within a few days Grant had the regiment encamped at Springfield, hard at work in the summer sun. Throughout the next few months, recruits poured in until Grant had nearly 20,000 men—who learned that he meant business. Each morning he had them up and marching at the crack of dawn. Laggards were forced to march in their stocking feet. They also learned that Grant cared little for showy display. When they first faced him on parade, their vociferous calls for a speech were met by a terse reply: "Men, go to your quarters."

When the Galena congressman requested advancement for his capable regimental commander, President Lincoln gave Grant, along with many others, a gold star. Grant wrote home that he was a general. His father wrote back to tell Ulysses that he finally had a good job now, and he'd better do his best to keep it.

Early in the war, Grant won two crucial victories on the western front. Launching simultaneous attacks by land and water, he first took Fort Henry on the Tennessee River, then Fort Donelson on the Cumberland, which was the gateway to Nashville. Penning up a group of rebels on the road out of Donelson to Nashville, Grant forced 15,000 of them to lay down their arms with a simple ultimatum that electrified the North. "No terms except unconditional and immediate surrender can be accepted. I propose to move immediately and unconditionally upon your works."

Unconditional surrender. U.S. Grant. "Unconditional Surrender" Grant. Those words fit the temper of the time. The North was jubilant with patriotism. Grant's quiet way of getting results appealed to a Northern citizenry that was impatient with conceptual strategies and paper plans. He gave the country what it wanted—results—while lacking in arms, transportation, organization and supplies.

In less than a year, Grant had gone from obscure clerk to national hero. Ten months earlier he had been a family charity case, considered a deadbeat and a ne'er-do-well. Now he was leading victorious armies into war. Grant found himself the toast of the nation. News stories described him coolly smoking under fire. Admirers from all over the nation shipped him crates of cigars. Grant, of course, remained as he had always been. He issued no grand pronouncements and made no show.

But his troubles were not over. In early April of 1862, in Tennessee, a two-day conflict escalated into one of the fiercest and bloodiest battles in history—the battle of Shiloh. General Grant had pushed south along the Tennessee River to join General Don Carlos Buell's 20,000-man army and threaten the Confederate railroad center of Corinth, Mississippi. Grant was camped at Pittsburgh Landing on the Tennessee River. His invasion of Tennessee had practically cut the state in two. Now he was waiting for the army of General Buell to join him. Their combined forces were to plunge into the heart of Mississippi.

But Buell was late and 22 miles away. The commander of the western department of the Confederate army, Albert Sidney Johnston, saw no reason to wait. The two armies were evenly matched. Now was the time to attack and end Grant's invasion. Under the early morning assault launched by Johnston, the Union divisions were overrun and began to panic. By late morning, many of the Union troops had seen enough. Most did not stop running until they reached the Tennessee River. There thousands cowered beneath a bluff.

Grant's back was to the Tennessee, with no sign of Buell's army and nowhere else to go. The center of the Union line was bent back like a horseshoe. By nightfall, however, the firing had stopped. The carnage was sickening. Everywhere men lay in agony. Hogs fed on the dead.

Grant spent that night beneath a tree, rather than remain at his headquarters to listen to the screams of the wounded men. It was there that he was found by his good friend and most trusted lieutenant, William Tecumseh Sherman. "Well, Grant," Sherman said, "we've had the devil's own day, haven't we." "Yes," replied Grant. "Lick 'em tomorrow though."

The battle of Shiloh
(Library of Congress)

During the night Buell's army finally arrived. Never was the sight of reinforcements so welcome to Grant. At dawn a Union force more than twice the size of the enemy's army launched its attack. The Confederates fell back, counterattacked, then began to withdraw to Corinth. The Union held the field. On both sides, there were more casualties than there had been in all previous American wars combined.

Grant was subjected to criticism for Shiloh. His superior was Henry "Old Brains" Halleck, a calculating administrator who had been jealous of Grant's earlier successes and anxious to rid himself of his chief rival. Old Brains spread rumors that Grant had been drunk at Shiloh; that was why Johnston had surprised him.

The fact is, Grant had kept away from whiskey ever since returning from the West to Julia and the children. But once a drunk, always a drunk, in the eyes of gossips. Grant's reward for the costly Union victory at Shiloh was to be removed from field command. Once again, the fortunes of his military career had plummeted.

Given the title of second-in-command, Grant was assigned no duties. He decided to quit the army altogether, but his friend Sherman talked him out of it. "You could not be quiet at home for a week, when armies are moving," Sherman said. Grant took the advice but stayed on the western front while critical battles of the war raged elsewhere, in faraway Virginia and Maryland.

During the remainder of 1862, Grant studied military maps. What he saw of greatest significance was the Confederate city of Vicksburg, Mississippi, a mighty fortress on top of a bluff over-looking the Mississippi River. The fortress was guarded by tens of thousands of bristling rebel artillerymen, but Grant could see that it had to be taken. It was a vital transportation hub of critical importance to holding the South together.

President Lincoln had been studying the same maps as Grant, and Lincoln had come to the same conclusion. Against the advice of his counselors, Lincoln reinstated Grant to field command. "I can't spare this man," Lincoln said in Washington. "He fights."

Late in 1862, Grant's first attempt to capture the Confederate stronghold called for a two-pronged attack by separate wings of his army, one headed by himself and the other by General Sherman. Grant's part in the campaign was to preoccupy Southern troops in northern Mississippi so that the bluffs north of Vicksburg, the key to the city, could not be reinforced. But his supply base was destroyed by raiding cavalry, and he was forced to withdraw.

The following year, Grant continued to hammer away at the Confederate stronghold. For two-and-a-half months, he doggedly attempted to dig or hack or float his army through the tangled bayous along the Mississippi River. Nothing worked. The press accused him of sloth and stupidity and openly suspected that he was drinking again.

Finally, he decided upon a daring plan. He would march downriver through the swamps on the western side and cross the river below Vicksburg. Once across, and without hope of resupply or reinforcement, he would come up from behind and attack the city.

Nothing that was not essential was taken ashore when Grant finally crossed the river with 30,000 troops. The Union soldiers knew they were cut loose from any reinforcements and had only a tenuous supply line. But Grant himself gave them confidence. They believed he knew what he was doing. His constant presence reassured them. Quite often on the march, by night or day, they saw him on his horse, spurring them to move on and close up ranks.

In Washington, Old Brains Halleck got word of Grant's movements and ordered him to desist. Grant ignored the order, stuffing away the telegram in his pocket. In three weeks, Grant's army, cut off from all communication with the outside world, marched 180 miles. They fought and won five battles. Finally, they surrounded Vicksburg itself, trapping 31,000 Confederates.

In one charge, they made it as far as the walls of the Confederate fort but, unable to force a breakthrough, were eventually repulsed, losing 1,000 men. Grant settled in for a siege, resolved, he said, "to outcamp the enemy," which had somehow managed to hold on.

Every day from late May, Grant's 200 Union guns pounded Vicksburg from land while gunboats battered it from the river. The shattering rain of shells continued day and night. Food ran low, and the city's defenders were reduced to eating horses, mules, and dogs. Grant's blockade of Vicksburg went on for so long that, here, he did take to the bottle out of boredom. Finally, after 48 days of siege, Vicksburg fell. It was a fitting day for celebration— July 4, 1863.

From then on, Grant's job was secure with the president. In March of 1864, he was ordered to Washington to receive his commission as lieutenant general commanding the armies of the United States. The rank of lieutenant general had been revived through a bill passed by Congress. Only one man had held it before—George Washington. As for the three stars, Grant later said there was only one soldier in the United States he took pleasure in outranking, the commander who had run him out of the army at Fort Humboldt 10 years before.

Prior to being ordered to Washington, Grant had planned to stay in the western states and lead the campaign against Atlanta, the industrial hub of the Deep South. But the talk in Washington was of the formidable brilliance of Confederate General Robert E. Lee.

The very mention of Lee's name still stirred fear in Washington. But Lee's fortunes had peaked. During the same week that Grant had seized Vicksburg, Lee's second invasion of the North had been stopped at Gettysburg. The South could never replace the manpower lost at the Pennsylvania battle. Together with Vicksburg, Gettysburg had marked the zenith of Confederate success.

Still, six other generals who had gone after Lee had come howling back in full retreat. Now Grant would go after the North's most pernicious nuisance. He would personally oversee the drive of the Army of the Potomac against Lee's Army of Northern Virginia, while Sherman was asked to lead the campaign against Atlanta.

It was Grant's turn, and he would try out his master plan of simultaneous pressure on all Southern armies. Unable to reinforce itself, Grant felt, the South would eventually exhaust its limited supply of manpower, especially if Lee were shadowed and hounded everywhere he went. Grant's strategy was to exhaust Lee's feared Army of Northern Virginia. "Lee's army will be your objective point," he told his generals. "Wherever Lee goes, you will go also."

It was early May of 1864, and Grant said he intended to fight it out with Lee if it took all summer. As Lee sideslipped to the south, Grant tailed him with an army three times the size of the Confederate force. Grant, heading east and south, kept probing to find Lee's weak points.

Grant maneuvered behind Petersburg to cut off Lee's southern supply line. Every step now was leading to victory for Grant. Still he proceeded with caution. He worried that Lee would escape to the Virginia interior and thence south to North Carolina when spring came. To prevent this, Grant had settled in for the long siege of Petersburg.

Grant's strategy was working. He had accomplished what had eluded all other Union commanders. For the first time, a Northern general had maneuvered Lee into a fixed position. Lee was pinned. The problem was to keep him pinned. Outside Petersburg the siege continued.

General Grant standing outside his field tent as the end of the war nears.
(National Archives)

The rebel enemy was now starving in its trenches, desperately in need of food and transportation. The rate of Federal fire increased. In April, a final Union assault caused Lee's defenses to crumble. The remnants of the Army of Northern Virginia withdrew from Petersburg, and on the morning of April 3 the city was in Grant's hands.

Lee began his final retreat. Grant followed closely behind, sending flanking troops around and in front of Lee's army. Squarely across Lee's front line of retreat, near a little village called Appomattox Courthouse, Grant's Army of the Potomac lay in wait. Lee was now surrounded, front, rear, and flank. When a rebel courier rode toward the Union armies, carrying a white flag of surrender, the game was up.

In a modest home at Appomattox Courthouse, Grant came in with half a dozen lieutenants. Scrubby and dirty in his mud-spattered boots, he greeted Lee. The contrast between the two commanders was astounding. One was short and awkward, both in appearance and in manner; the other tall, handsome, well-groomed. But there was no personal enmity between them.

Like so many others in both North and South, Grant greatly admired Lee. Clearly uncomfortable in accepting victory, Grant made small talk for awhile about both of them having served in the Mexican War. It was Grant's gracious way of trying to soften the weight of defeat. But both men knew what they were there for.

Grant took out his pen. He later confessed that he had no idea what he was going to write. Then he scribbled one of the most important sentences in American history. The Southerners could go home, he wrote, "not to be disturbed by the United States authorities so long as they observe their paroles and the laws in force where they may reside." Those words made it impossible for the government of the United States to exact punishment from any Southerners whom it considered traitors.

The surrender of the Southern armies put an end to the military conflict. In Washington, the city was wildly celebrating the victory. Buildings were illuminated, bands played, and, across the Potomac River, 1,000 slaves gathered on the grounds of what had been Lee's estate to sing the "Year of Jubilee."

In Washington for the victory celebration, Grant met with Lincoln and his cabinet. He and Julia planned to join the President and the First Lady in a visit to the theater on April 14. At the last minute, however, there was a change of plans. Ever after, Grant wondered what would have happened had he been in Ford's Theater that evening. It was the night that Lincoln was assassinated.

A year after the war, Grant became the first full four-star general in American history. He now outranked George Washington. As the army's top general, he went on trips with Julia and gave parties at his new home in Washington. He refused to make speeches, and no one knew where he stood on the great questions of the day, postwar treatment of the Southern states and black suffrage.

Yet, in spite of his desire to stay in the military, Grant found himself embroiled in the bitter controversies of the Reconstruction period. These problems he was not equipped to deal with, either by temperament or training. President Andrew Johnson made him secretary of war. In that capacity, Grant recommended that General Lee receive amnesty. Failing that, Grant refused to execute Johnson's order to arrest Lee, who had been indicted by a federal grand jury on charges of treason.

"When can these men be tried?" Johnson asked Grant of Lee and Jefferson Davis. "Never," said Grant. "Never, unless they violate their paroles. I have made certain terms with Lee," he added. "The best and only terms. I will resign the command of the army rather than execute any order directing me to arrest Lee."

Nothing else was ever said about Lee's indictment. But the incident left a bad taste in Grant's mouth. At his inauguration as President of the United States in 1869, Grant would not even sit in the same carriage with outgoing President Johnson.

Grant regarded his own election to the presidency as no more than a natural promotion from his job as four-star general. As head of the nation, he remained as modest and shy as ever; his inaugural address was barely heard beyond the first few rows of listeners.

Although the policies he advocated during his two terms in office were sound, Grant never learned the art of which Lincoln was the supreme master, that of using the selfish ambitions of men to accomplish great and patriotic purposes. Within six months, he had lost control of his staff in a major scandal. His administration had become enmeshed in a scheme by profiteers to corner the gold supply of the United States. Half his staff had profited on the deal. Grant had not.

The news led to a stock market crash that ruined hundreds of speculating firms and thousands of individuals. Another big loser was Grant himself, when it was whispered that his wife had made money on the deal, which she had not. But these scandals did not diminish the confidence that the voters had in Grant. He won an even easier victory over his Democratic opponent, Horace Greeley, in the election of 1872.

After leaving the White House in 1877, Grant was involved in a number of unprofitable business ventures. Filing bankruptcy in 1884, he faced one more descent into misfortune, a hopeless struggle with a cancerous growth in his throat. Mustering his remaining energies, he spent the last year of his life writing his personal memoirs.

The fascinating self-portrait was Grant's final victory. No less a literary authority than Mark Twain called the memoirs "the best of any general's since Caesar." They sold a million copies, twice as many as Twain's *Huckleberry Finn*, and Grant's bankrupt family was returned to prosperity.

Grant will always be remembered first and foremost for doing what the half-dozen generals who preceded him were unable to do. He forced Lee to fight on Union terms, and he brought him to surrender. What helped him to succeed where others had failed? Certainly he had his flaws. But he had flashes of great genius as well. If Shiloh revealed him at his worst, Vicksburg brought out his flawless best. It was one of the most brilliant military operations in American history.

Despite the genius of battles like Vicksburg, Grant's brilliance as a military strategist was overshadowed by his strength of character. For all that he plainly was, shy, diffident, physically unimpressive—he had tremendous strength of character. Unlike so many other Union commanders who came before him, he rarely complained. He simply went ahead and did the job with the resources at hand. "I don't believe in strategy in the popular understanding of the term," Grant once admitted. "I use it to get just as close to the enemy as practicable with as little loss as possible. Then, up guards, and at 'em."

William McFeely, in an introduction to Grant's autobiography, explains why Grant was so successful in doing the amazing things he did. "He saw conflict simply, and it is perhaps this simple fact that led him to be the great strategist he was," said McFeely. "He was the unusual man who in normal times was incapable of raising himself above the mass. But when things were at their worst and an abnormal situation arose, he rose with it, keeping his head, learning his lessons, and coming through."

Chronology

April 27, 1822	born at Point Pleasant, Ohio
June 1843	graduates from West Point
August 22, 1848	marries Julia Dent
1852	departs for Panama
September 1853	transferred to Humboldt Bay
July 1854	resigns from army
August 1861	made brigadier general
February 1862	captures Fort Henry and Fort Donelson
April 6–10, 1862	battle of Shiloh
July 4, 1863	captures Vicksburg
March 1864	promoted to lieutenant general
April 3, 1865	captures Richmond
April 9, 1865	Lee surrenders to Grant
1866	general of the U.S. armies
1867	appointed Secretary of War
January 1869	inaugurated U.S. President
November 1872	reelected for second term
July 23, 1885	dies at Mount McGregor, N.Y.

Further Reading

Fuller, J. F. C. *The Generalship of Ulysses S. Grant*. New York: Da Capo Press, 1991. A well-researched examination of Grant's military abilities.

Grant, Ulysses S. *Personal Memoirs*. New York: Charles L. Webster, 1894; first published 1885–86. Grant's personal memoirs have come to be regarded as one of the great autobiographies in American literature.

Porter, Horace. *Campaigning with Grant*. New York: Da Capo Press, 1986. A first-hand account of Grant's campaigns, with a new introduction by William S. McFeely.

Smith, Gene. *Lee and Grant*. New York: Meridian, 1984. An extremely well-written dual biography of Grant and Robert E. Lee.

James Longstreet
Lee's Warhorse

James Longstreet
(Library of Congress)

*R*ather than the Southern war hero that he unquestionably was, James Longstreet was cast in the role of villain by his own Confederacy when it went down in defeat. Yet as the senior lieutenant general of the entire Confederate army, General Lee's "warhorse" was a tremendous asset to the Army of Northern Virginia in the War Between the States.

After the war, Longstreet joined the Republican Party, served as President Grant's minister to Turkey, and dared to criticize the Confederate strategy at Gettysburg. For this he was severely criticized in the war of words that followed the peace. His former military colleagues accused him of disloyalty and having lost the battle of Gettysburg.

Much of the criticism totally ignored the outstanding service that Longstreet rendered to the Confederate cause. Today Longstreet is remembered as a steadfast corps commander who held out until the bitter end, not once even suggesting that surrender be considered.

James Longstreet was born in Edgefield, South Carolina, January 8, 1821, the fifth of 11 children. His ancestors had come from New Jersey and were of Dutch extraction. His father and namesake, who had come to South Carolina to farm in the fertile South, died when James was 12 years old. His mother moved to the vicinity of Augusta, Georgia. Soon afterward she moved again, to nearby Huntsville. There Longstreet was reared by his uncle, Judge Augustus Baldwin Longstreet, brother to the future general's father.

Judge Longstreet served chiefly as president of Emory College in Atlanta, and later of other Southern universities. One of the leading Southerners of the time, he had a strong influence on the cultural life of the South, not only as a jurist and educator, but also as a humorist and author of *Georgia Scenes*, one of the most influential books of the antebellum period.

The judge's contribution to his nephew's character was greater than that of anyone else outside the immediate family, even though he had little time for James. Under his uncle's guardianship, James was often alone during his formative years on the plantation. He was a mischievous sort and animated with a spirit of levity that blended well with his natural love of the great outdoors.

James liked to pass his time on horseback, or hunting and fishing, and these skills were an important benefit to his later years as a soldier. Uppermost in his mind, at an early age in fact, was the desire to become a soldier. He enjoyed reading about military heroes, especially Caesar, Alexander the Great, Napoleon, and, of course, Washington. Perhaps he was destined to become the future "Old War Horse" of Civil War fame. There wasn't much else that held his interest. Other than military history, he was not the studious type.

James attended school in Somerville, Alabama, where his mother had moved. At his uncle's urging, he studied enough to qualify for the entrance exam to the United States Military Academy, and was admitted to West Point from the state of Alabama.

71

A cousin in that state, who happened to be a member of Congress, helped him win the appointment.

During a stopover in New York City, en route to West Point in the summer of 1838, two street urchins gave James a fictitious story of their father's death, hoping to extract money for transportation to his "funeral." New to the city and its ways, James sympathetically gave in, but a policeman approached just in time to frighten off the young swindlers and preserve his finances.

As a student at West Point, Longstreet did not do well academically. But the green country boy did everything ably that called for physical exertion, sports, and horsemanship. He was six-feet-two-inches tall, with dark brown hair and blue eyes—and good-looking enough to be voted the handsomest cadet at West Point. He later confessed that his nonscholastic activities such as riding had lifted his average enough for him to graduate. One year behind him was his good friend Ulysses S. Grant, the man who would wring defeat from Longstreet's army under General Robert E. Lee more than 20 years later.

"Dutch," as his schoolmates called him, or "Old Pete," graduated in 1842 near the bottom of his class, 54th in a class of 62, and he was assigned to the Fourth Infantry at Jefferson Barracks, Missouri, near St. Louis. Jefferson Barracks was then a famous western military post, and James enjoyed life there. On the outskirts of town lived relatives from his mother's side of the family. Also assigned to Jefferson Barracks was his old school chum, Grant. Old Pete introduced Grant to his cousin, Julia Dent, and the two were soon married. The friendship between Grant and Longstreet ripened and lasted through the years following the Civil War.

The young Lieutenant Longstreet was then sent to Fort Jessup in Louisiana. There he served under the old Indian fighter General Zachary Taylor, and then with the 8th Infantry at St. Augustine, Florida. At this time the Mexican War was about to break out. In March 1846, Longstreet was ordered with Taylor's forces to the Rio Grande at Matamoros.

Across the fenceless plains of Texas the column of soldiers moved, soon entering Mexico. Many of the sentries and single soldiers were shot at by Mexican snipers. Small skirmishes took place frequently between the American and Mexicans. Longstreet himself saw hot action at Molino del Rey, a hard-fought battle in which the Americans suffered considerable losses. But Longstreet himself came through without a scratch. At the great Mexican fortress of Chapultepec, he was not so lucky. There he was shot through the thigh while carrying the regimental flag. The city's defenses were now in American hands, though, and the invaders had all but taken Mexico City.

Longstreet returned home with a month's leave. In March of 1848 he wedded Marie Louis Garland, the daughter of his former brigade commander. The ceremony took place at Lynchburg, Virginia. It seems to have been a happy marriage. It was certainly a fruitful one, for 10 children were born to the couple.

Longstreet found himself back in Jefferson Barracks by the autumn of 1848. He remained with this regiment for some years, serving in the Indian campaigns in the West until 1855. In that year he took a transfer to become a major in the paymaster department at Albuquerque, New Mexico Territory. Longstreet had bidden his farewell to arms, giving up all hope of military glory. The better pay, important to the head of a growing family, was probably the deciding factor.

Longstreet's fellow officers at Albuquerque were a congenial group who spent most of their time together amidst the alien population of ex-Mexican Hispanics. There were regular games of poker, with Longstreet winning his share of the pots. A mixture of Northerners and Southerners, they all hoped against hope that civil war could be averted. But the politicians could not come up with an acceptable compromise.

When news arrived of the bombardment of Fort Sumter, Longstreet's fellow officers tried to persuade him to keep his position in the U.S. Army. Longstreet sent in his resignation, silencing his fellow officers with the argument, "What would you do if your state seceded?"

His biggest concern at the time seemed to be his separation from the army's payroll. Already he was planning to become paymaster of the new Confederate government. He set out in a stagecoach for El Paso, Texas, where he parted from his wife and family, and made for the Confederate capital at Richmond, Virginia.

Arriving there, he found that West Point graduates were in great demand. Longstreet's own background was considered too valuable to be squandered doling out monthly paychecks. Right away he was commissioned as brigadier general, and shipped out to the front at Manassas Station in Virginia.

Longstreet's troops knew their commander had a solid reputation. His silence and self-confidence gave him an air of complete reliability. "Old Pete," as his soldiers called him, was slightly deaf, but he was a dignified man, who never seemed to tire. Had those who knew him well been asked to describe him in one word, they might well have agreed on the same soldierly term—reliable.

His calm imperturbability in battle was first exhibited at Bull Run, a small stream that flows into Occoquan Creek, which empties a short run later into the Potomac River not far from the nation's capital. The odds there were fairly even, except that the Union artillery was incomparably better equipped. Longstreet's troops received their baptism of fire when rifle balls and shell fragments began to fly among them.

Longstreet was unaffected. He played it all with a poker face. When part of his line broke, he rode straight into battle with his saber in hand, determined to rally his men. After rallying from their initial panic, Longstreet's 1,200 men stood their ground and repelled the Union attack. The engagement ended as the Union troops realized that the front at Bull Run could not be broken without a slaughter on both sides. Longstreet had revealed his greatest military quality, which was his talent for defensive tactics.

He had badly wanted to open fire on the retreating Yankees. But an initial order to do so was rescinded. He was sorely disappointed. It had been a great victory. And he had been there on the field, ready for anything. But the opportunity for glory had not come to him. He had done as much as any other general, except for Stonewall Jackson, who won instant fame as the hero of Bull Run.

The army was now stationed near Centreville. Longstreet's men were eager to press forward to more victories. But the Confederate army did nothing at that point but drill and erect earthworks. They were preparing to repel an attack, not launch one. Longstreet himself had no qualms with the defensive strategy. He sat and waited for the enemy to come. It always seemed preferable to him to wait and hold out in some strong position rather than to attack.

By August, Longstreet was commanding the "Advanced Forces," a mixed body of infantry and cavalry. Thrust ahead of the Confederate position to observe the enemy, he made a striking impression on his superiors. It was the effect that self-confidence usually has, and Longstreet had unlimited confidence in himself. When the rank of major general was established in the Confederate army, Longstreet was among the first five commissioned.

By the following May, Major General George McClellan's Union army had worked its way up the Richmond Peninsula, between the York and James rivers, to within six miles of the Confederate capital of Richmond, Virginia. Longstreet suggested an attack on the Union center at Seven Pines. It seemed a great opportunity. Parts of the Union army were divided by an impassable barrier—the rising Chickahominy River. If the Confederates could move quickly, one wing of the Union army might be destroyed before aid could come from the other wing.

Longstreet attacked first. For several hours the battle raged on a front of about two miles. Through the flooded woods the rebels swarmed, finally driving the Army of the Potomac from its defenses. But the Confederate army suffered severe losses and broke down in disorder. By the end of the day, the Union army was stronger than it had been at the beginning of the battle. The next day, as had happened the day before, confusion hindered the Confederate attack. Longstreet commanded only two brigades. This weak attack was easily repulsed and concluded the battle of Seven Pines at Fair Oaks.

Tactically the battle was a draw. But strategically it was a Confederate defeat. Longstreet was partly to blame. He had succeeded in getting only a fraction of the force into battle. His tardiness in taking an offensive position was considered a material factor in the Confederate failure.

In June, General Robert E. Lee was placed in command of the Army of Northern Virginia. Three weeks later, Longstreet was invited to join a council of war at Lee's headquarters. Lee chose to make a combined attack on the Union position north of the Chickahominy in what became known as the Seven Days' Battle.

All along the line, the Confederates rushed up the hillside, disregarding the awful hail of bullets and canister that swept their ranks. Longstreet deployed his troops across fields spotted with dense woods. Advancing through the woods and across open spaces, he speedily came to grips with the Union troops. His men swept forward until the lines of blue and gray intermingled. A fierce melee with bayonets and gun butts sent Longstreet's forces back with heavy losses. As the day's shadows lengthened, his worn troops were reinforced with fresh men. The Yankees began to withdraw during the night. About 12,000 men had fallen on both sides.

Longstreet then prevailed upon Lee to pursue Union General McClellan to Malvern Hill. "Don't get scared, now that we have got him licked," he told Lee. Yet because of the thick forest, Longstreet was able to find ground for only a few artillery guns. These were blown to pieces the moment they opened fire on the massed Union batteries on the hill. This bloody defeat brought an end to the campaign, and McClellan accomplished his withdrawal.

Now that the Confederates at Richmond had a breathing spell, they began to fight the Seven Days' Battle all over again—in the newspapers. Longstreet had basked in the light of glory for some days, when an article appeared in *The Richmond Examiner* attributing to General A. P. Hill much of the credit for forcing the Union withdrawal.

Since Hill ranked under Longstreet, the latter's jealous nature flared up at once. He had a reply printed in *The Richmond Whig* that was uncomplimentary to Hill. When Hill thereupon refused to have anything to do with Longstreet, Longstreet put him under arrest. The problem was resolved when Hill was transferred, but the incident reflected poorly on Longstreet.

In August, Longstreet met with Lee and Stonewall Jackson to devise a plan for confronting the new Northern army under the command of Major General John Pope. Before a campfire, they mapped out the line along the Rappahannock and Rapidan rivers. If the Confederate cavalry could be thrown across the Rapidan before Pope knew what was going on, the Union commander would be trapped between the rivers and might be destroyed.

The element of timing would be all-important. Lee had to defeat Pope before his army could link up with McClellan's. If the two Union armies united, the Confederates would be forced to fall back to Richmond. Longstreet suggested a maneuver around the right side of Pope's army, which was concentrated at Manassas Junction.

Longstreet accompanied Lee to the summit of Clark's Mountain, an isolated elevation near Orange Courthouse. There, between the two rivers, they saw the flag of Pope's army floating placidly above the tops of the trees. Hearing of a stir in the Union camp, Longstreet rode again with Lee to the top of the mountain. Lines of wagons, 15 miles away, were in motion. Having learned of the approach of Longstreet's 30,000-man division, Pope was escaping from the trap, just as it was about to close in on him.

Advancing to the south bank of the Rappahannock River, Longstreet came into contact with Union pickets and artillery fire across the river, at Rappahannock Bridge. Longstreet unleashed his own artillery fire as if preparing to cross there, but there was no battle. He was merely demonstrating his firepower in order to distract the enemy from observing Jackson, who had formed his battle line in the woods behind an unfinished railroad embankment.

Longstreet was slow in crossing the Rapidan, but it did not matter. When Pope's army discovered Jackson in the woods, and turned away from the Rappahannock, Longstreet decided to move up the river. That afternoon his troops began their march on a round-about route. He was slow in starting the following morning, and further delayed by the appearance of Union cavalry. The end of his second day of riding found him miles short of Jackson's infantry.

Finally Longstreet came to the northern end of Thoroughfare Gap, a pass in the low and lovely Bull Run Mountains, which form a spur of the Blue Ridge Mountains. Longstreet cleared the gap and galloped off to meet Jackson at Manassas Junction. There the whole Union army was bearing down on Jackson. As Longstreet rode east the crackle of artillery fire sounded louder and louder. His men quickened step, filing down the turnpike and joining Jackson not a moment too soon. The Second Battle of Manassas, one of the most remarkable battles of modern history, was already raging when Longstreet arrived on Jackson's right.

Lee was anxious for Longstreet to assume the offensive that day. But Longstreet, always cautious and deliberate in attack, made repeated excuses for not doing so. Finally, on the following day, Longstreet attacked and caught the charging Union masses off guard. The surprised Yankees halted, wavered, and began to fall back. Jackson was saved from slaughter.

Then Longstreet sent five more divisions storming into the Union flank. The charge was splendidly made. But masses of bewildered Yankees did not give way at first. Knots of men held on in a severe struggle. Finally the Union lines broke. Longstreet swept on, driving the enemy back. Overwhelmed, there was nothing for Pope to do but retreat. Twenty-five thousand were killed, captured or wounded at Second Manassas, five times the number of First Manassas one year earlier.

The outlook of the war had now changed startlingly. Not long before, Richmond had been in danger. Now Washington itself was imperiled. The North was on the defensive. Yet Longstreet was dissatisfied and critical. In his military autobiography, he later spoke of the errors of the battle of Second Manassas, committed by Lee and Jackson. Longstreet, of course, never committed errors. At least he admitted to no errors on his own part.

With the fortunes of the North at low ebb, the Confederate government set its sights on Maryland. It was determined to invade and to bring the war to Northern soil. Longstreet did not endorse the expedition into Maryland. As usual, he attempted to dissuade Lee from advancing and showed his disinclination for fighting except on the defensive. But he fought well when the battle was finally joined at Antietam Creek in mid-September.

Longstreet's command took position in front of the little town of Sharpsburg, two miles north of the Potomac River at Shepherdstown. The following afternoon, Federal troops pushed forward across the Antietam Creek. The battle of Antietam, one of the bloodiest conflicts in American military history, opened at daylight.

Longstreet held the right side of the Confederate line. He knew that if the Northerners broke through there, the Army of Northern Virginia would be cut in two and probably destroyed. Relying on his tactical skills in defense, he shifted his troops from point to point as needed. He himself was exposed to fire, but seemed never to know the meaning of physical fear.

At one point, all his artillery gunners had been killed or wounded. Longstreet ordered his staff officers to the guns while he held their horses. The officers sent a rattle of shells into the charging Yankees as they came up over the crest of a hill. The Yankees fell back and the position was held. The sun set on the Confederate army still clinging to the same position it had held that morning.

The battle of Antietam
(Library of Congress)

As darkness fell on the field, Longstreet rode along aiding in the rescue of the wounded. The carnage was terrible. Everywhere men lay groaning from severed limbs. At headquarters, as Longstreet wearily dismounted, Lee came up to him and put two affectionate hands on his shoulders. "Here is my old warhorse at last," Lee said.

The battle was finally over. The Confederates recrossed the Potomac River into Virginia. They had held their ground against all assaults, but had come out of Maryland badly bruised and disheartened. For Longstreet, the battle marked a critical stage in his development. He was filled with a sense of futility at the battle he had advised against from the very start. Writing years later, he passed harsh judgment on Lee's generalship at Antietam. Of course, Lee was long dead when the charges appeared.

For now, Longstreet kept his opinions to himself. On Lee's recommendation, in October of 1862, he was made lieutenant general. Two months later, the whole Union army, now under Major General Ambrose Burnside, made a swift march to Falmouth, a town across the Rappahannock River from Fredericksburg, Virginia. Longstreet snuck in behind the picturesque Virginia town, after Burnside had taken possession of it. The town, now deserted by most of its inhabitants, was surrounded by rebels.

Longstreet and the rest of the Confederate line were established on the high ground west of Fredericksburg. The seven-mile line included a strong position where Southern artillery gunners stood in a sunken road behind a stone wall, with more artillery massed on Marye's Heights above them.

As it turned out, the great Union force had little stomach for what appeared a hopeless venture. After several fruitless and costly Union charges, the Confederate artillery atop the hill blew holes in the advancing Union columns. Longstreet's artillery gunners in the sunken road mowed down wave after wave of bluecoats. The attacks were suicidal; none of the Northerners got within 20 yards of the stone wall. Darkness finally ended the slaughter.

Two days later, under cover of darkness and a heavy rain, Burnside's Army of the Potomac recrossed the Rappahannock River. Fredericksburg, with its heavy cost to the Union and its much smaller loss for the Confederates, was Longstreet's ideal battle. He had performed well, handling his part of the Confederate line better than Stonewall Jackson had his, and had fought from a strongly held defensive position.

Longstreet's reputation was as high then as it would ever be in his military career. But his personal life was at low ebb. In January of 1863, he answered a hurried summons from his wife, rushed to Richmond, and returned a changed, unhappy man. Scarlet fever, which had been epidemic in the city, had taken the lives of three of his children. Shaken by his grief, he became less communicative. After that tragic January, he was a soldier and little else, absorbed tirelessly in his duty.

Now Longstreet also became wearier of serving under Lee. He fancied himself in the role of supreme commander, and was elated when fate finally threw the chance his way. The Confederate government had become worried about North Carolina. The long coastline of that state exposed it to Union raids by sea. Richmond authorities also were increasingly concerned about guarding the roads to Richmond from the south and east. With North Carolina fearful and Richmond nervous, Longstreet was granted his long-desired opportunity to exercise his first independent command.

In February his division followed two others to southeastern Virginia for the so-called "Suffolk Campaign," but no substantial achievement of any sort resulted. Although his force equaled that of the Northerners, he failed to seize the initiative. For some reason, he was content to employ his troops in collecting supplies from eastern North Carolina.

Lee diplomatically urged him either to fight or rejoin the Army of Northern Virginia. But Lee was at a distance from Longstreet and without precise knowledge of his difficulties. Lee refrained from giving him peremptory orders. The result was that Longstreet neither fought nor returned. The absence of two of his divisions was the chief reason Lee could not follow up on the victory he won against Major General Joseph Hooker at Chancellorsville in early May.

That battle had one other tragic consequence. It claimed the life of Stonewall Jackson. After Jackson's death, Longstreet became Lee's most distinguished lieutenant. He began to take it upon himself to act as Lee's mentor. He suggested that the invasion of Pennsylvania, which Lee was then planning, should be defensive in tactics. And he was somehow left with the mistaken idea that Lee had made him a promise to this effect.

When Longstreet joined Lee at Gettysburg in July, he was disappointed to learn that Lee intended to attack. Longstreet appeared disgruntled and filled with misgivings and premonitions of failure. The story of Gettysburg, as it concerns Longstreet, is the story of his slow and despairing acquiescence in orders he believed would bring disaster.

Longstreet delayed action until it was too late to execute Lee's plan to storm Cemetery Ridge before it was fully manned. With that delay, Longstreet made a disastrous attack on July 3 almost a military necessity. The clear disadvantages that convinced Longstreet it was dangerous for Lee to assume the offensive were aggravated by Longstreet's own tardiness and lack of confidence.

Gettysburg virtually concluded Longstreet's service with the Army of Northern Virginia during the period of its major offensive operations. In the lull following Gettysburg, in September 1863, he was dispatched to Georgia with two divisions to fight under the command of General Braxton Bragg. Longstreet achieved spectacular results at the Confederate victory at Chickamauga, in Georgia, where he unleashed a series of savage assaults against Union General George Thomas. It was the only great victory won by the South in the Western theater during the entire war.

After that battle, while the siege of Chattanooga was in progress, Bragg ordered Longstreet into Tennessee to take on his old foe, Union General Burnside, who had occupied Knoxville. Isolated in eastern Tennessee, Longstreet became frustrated with his failure to capture Knoxville. He was so close to despair, in fact, that he contemplated resignation. Aroused, however, by the imminent danger of a Northern invasion of Georgia, Longstreet proposed several plans for an offensive in Tennessee and Kentucky. None of these was accepted by Confederate President Jefferson Davis.

Old Pete and his troops were finally brought back to Virginia, where they were needed most, in April 1864. He was stationed near Gordonsville, however, too far to the south to participate in the opening skirmishes of the battle of the Wilderness. Longstreet led a forced march and arrived just as the Confederate line was breaking under the severe pounding of Grant's superior numbers. He helped stop the Union advance, then organized a counterattack that threw the Union lines into confusion. Just as he was issuing his instructions for continuing the attack, he was accidentally hit by fire from his own men and severely wounded.

Longstreet was not fit for full duty until late in the fall, and even then his right arm was paralyzed. By fall, the Confederate army was backed up against Richmond and Petersburg. While Grant slowly edged his way around Lee, Longstreet attempted to cover Lee's flanks. But the sheer force of numbers pushed Lee back. Richmond fell and the collapse of the Confederacy became inevitable.

After the war, Longstreet became the head of an insurance company and prospered for a time as a cotton farmer in New

Longstreet, the postwar Republican
(Library of Congress)

Orleans. He and Grant, who had last seen each other on the streets of St. Louis before the war, renewed their friendship. Longstreet also joined the Republican Party, the party of Abraham Lincoln, and was ostracized by his fellow Southerners as a result. His espousal of the Republican faith probably caused some post-bellum Southern writers to do him less than justice. The claims he made in his military autobiography only aggravated the feelings against him.

More than eight years after Gettysburg, Longstreet's fellow officers began to attack him for his role in that battle. The resulting damage to Longstreet's reputation continued until after his death on January 2, 1904. In various biographies, Longstreet was depicted as a kind of sulking malcontent who dragged his heels in battle.

Despite these unfair criticisms, his place in American military history is assured. Essentially a combat officer, he did not possess the qualities necessary for the success of his independent command, and his skill in strategy was not great.

His maneuvers were apt to be slow, and he was much too prone to await attack. But for resourcefulness in holding a defensive position, he was seldom surpassed. And once the battle was joined, he displayed a cheerful composure and skill in handling his troops that made him an ideal corps commander.

It wasn't until Douglas Southall Freeman's eloquent biography, *Lee's Lieutenants*, was published in 1946 that opinion changed. "Lee failed," said Freeman, "because of his own indecisions and wrong decisions, and not because Longstreet, or anyone else let him down."

Chronology

January 8, 1824	born in Edgefield, S.C.
July 1842	graduates West Point
March 8, 1848	marries Maria Louise Garland
July 19, 1858	promoted to major
June 1, 1861	resigns from army
June 17, 1861	joins Confederacy as brigadier general
May 31, 1862	battle of Seven Pines
June 25, 1862	Seven Days' Battle around Richmond
August 29, 1862	battle of Second Manassas
September 17, 1862	battle of Antietam
October 11, 1862	made lieutenant general
December 13, 1862	battle of Fredericksburg
July 3, 1863	battle of Gettysburg
September 1863	dispatched to Georgia
April 1864	returns to Virginia
May 6, 1864	battle of the Wilderness
September 8, 1897	marries Helen Dortch
January 2, 1904	dies in Gainesville, Georgia

Further Reading

Connelly, Thomas Lawrence, and Barbara Bellows. *God and General Longstreet: The Lost Cause and the Southern Mind.* Baton Rouge: Louisiana State University Press, 1982. A well-researched defense of Longstreet's role in the war.

Freeman, Douglas Southall. *Lee's Lieutenants, A Study In Command.* New York: C. Scribner's Sons, 1946. Acquitted Longstreet of blame given him for defeat of Lee at Gettysburg.

Longstreet, James. *From Manassas to Appomattox: Memoirs of the Civil War in America.* New York: Da Capo Press, 1992; first published, 1896. Longstreet's first-hand account of the Civil War, critical of decisions made by generals Lee and Jackson.

Piston, William Garrett. *Lee's Tarnished Lieutenant: James Longstreet and His Place in Southern History.* Athens: University of Georgia Press, 1987. A balanced examination of the controversy surrounding Longstreet's commitment to the Southern military cause.

Thomas J. Jackson
The Stone Wall

Thomas J. Jackson
(National Archives)

*N*either side in the Civil War had gained or lost much by the summer of 1861 until a Southern religious fanatic first glared out from his mangy old forage cap at the Northern invaders. Thomas Jackson had been an oddball professor at Virginia Military Institute in Lexington when the war broke out. He could easily have escaped notice for the rest of his life. But this humorless, fire-and-brimstone Presbyterian knew how to train cadets. Together they went on a series of ungodly slaughters, carried out with Old Testament fury, against the invading Yankee infidels in Virginia's Shenandoah Valley.

If Jackson showed no mercy with the enemy, he showed little more with his own men. A stern disciplinarian, he kept them marching all over the strategic Shenandoah. In no time his infantry could pop up anywhere, flying from place to place so swiftly that they became known as a "foot cavalry." Not once did Jackson lead his brigade to defeat, even against three armies at once. He seemed invincible to everyone, until he was accidentally shot down by one of his own men. Had Jackson lived, there's no telling how long the Confederacy could have held out.

Thomas Jackson was born on January 21, 1824, in Clarksburg, Virginia, a second son and third child. His Scot-Irish father, Jonathan Jackson, formed a cavalry company in the War of 1812. Relatives had served in the U.S. Congress, and his cousin, Judge John Jackson, was married to the sister of Dolly Madison. Everyone seemed to like Jonathan Jackson, even when he became the tax collector for western Virginia. He was a generous man, who dipped into his own pocket sometimes when others were short on tax payments.

Unfortunately, Jonathan's generosity left his family destitute when he died in 1827. Tom was only three years old then, but already death seemed to surround him. Jackson's father had nursed his older sister, Elizabeth, until her death of typhoid fever at age 11—and lay dead a month later of the same illness. It was March of 1826. The very next day his widow, Julia, gave birth to another girl. Tom's widowed mother now had two young sons and a newborn daughter to raise.

First Julia moved the family into a nearby cottage. There she ran a small school for a few pupils, until she found a new suitor. He was a lawyer, like her deceased husband, and like him he was also inept at family finances. When the family moved to Fayette County, Julia took ill. Tom was then sent to live with his grandmother at Jackson Mill, far out in the boondocks. He never saw his stepfather again.

At Jackson Mill, Tom's Uncle Cummins was the head of the household. He was a big man, over six feet tall and a perennial bachelor. He took Tom under his wing, and the two of them often

87

went creek-bank fishing together. Uncle Cummins liked fights and race horses, too, anything where there was gambling involved. He would sometimes saddle up young Tom on his racing ventures. Tom was no great rider, but he was sturdy in the saddle.

In 1831 Tom's mother sent for all her children. She was seriously ill, after just giving birth to Tom's stepbrother. She wanted to see her children for the last time. Tom was only seven, but he knew all too well that death was knocking on his family's door again.

Tom's older brother Warren had a big influence on him, especially after the death of their mother. One autumn morning the two set off together in a raft down the Ohio River. The pair returned months later, both bone-thin, with coughs and fevers. Warren's coughing persisted. By the time he was 19, Warren had passed on.

While he was still an adolescent, Tom was sent by his Uncle Cummins to a private school at the local courthouse. There he was taught by a justice of the peace and military historian who saw something special in him. He helped Tom win appointment as county constable, his first steady job, at age 17.

While constable, Tom continued to study. In 1842, he tried but failed to win an appointment to West Point. He had been edged out by a brighter young man who, as it turned out, resigned after a change of heart about the rigors of military life. Jackson, the runner-up, was tapped as a substitute. At age 18, he entered the gates of West Point wearing a weatherbeaten felt cap. All of his worldly belongings were packed in a pair of saddlebags. The backwoods were written all over him, but he had left the frontier forever.

Much handicapped by his poor preliminary education, Tom "studied very hard," by his own admission. He was so engrossed in his work that he said afterward he did not remember having spoken to a single woman during his whole cadetship. While he rose steadily in his grades, year by year, he was always behind. His persistence paid off when he graduated near the top of his class. His classmates nicknamed him "the General" after Andrew Jackson. By his fourth year, a joke went around his class of cadets. "If the General could stay here another year, he'd be number one in the class."

At 22 years old, Jackson left West Point, a breveted second lieutenant of artillery. It was June of 1846, and he had a war to go to in Mexico. Serving as a lieutenant in "Prince John" Magruder's battery, Jackson killed four Mexicans in hand-to-hand combat at

La Jolla, and took three prisoners. Then he almost singlehandedly held off the Mexican cavalry, firing light cannon from a hilltop, while others scaled a massive wall at the fortress of Chapultepec near Mexico City. The victory at Chapultepec opened the way for the army to enter and occupy Mexico City, ending the war. In July 1848, Jackson returned from Mexico to the United States.

Back home, Jackson settled down to the comparatively dull routine of garrison life. He was first stationed at Carlisle, Pennsylvania, on the barrack's court-martial board. Then he was transferred to Fort Hamilton on Long Island, 10 miles outside New York. Jackson loved New York. An avid reader, on trips to the city he would spend hours in the bookstalls on Fourth Avenue.

For a while he toyed with the idea of leaving the military. Before long, however, he was transferred to the frontier in the new state of Florida, where there had been frequent wars against Seminole Indians in past decades. In Florida, at Fort Meade, Jackson's legendary stubbornness surfaced in an ugly episode with Major William Henry French. Trouble was brewing after a scouting team led by Jackson failed to find any Seminole Indians. French feared that the whole reason for the fort's existence could be called into question. He blamed Jackson, a convenient scapegoat. Soon rumors began circulating, started by Jackson, that French had an extramarital appetite for a young servant girl.

When French traced the rumors back to their source, he had Jackson thrown in the brig. Charges and countercharges swamped their superior generals. The ugly episode came to an end when Jackson was released from jail and French was transferred. Jackson immediately resigned. In May 1851 he left Fort Meade for a professorship in philosophy and artillery tactics at Virginia Military Institute.

Jackson was not especially successful as a teacher and was the butt of many a joke. To the young cadets there, he was known as "Old Jack" or "Tom Fool." They considered him something of a martinet and a stickler for regulations. They knew that he had graduated from West Point and had won some honors for his service in the Mexican War. But to their youthful minds, all that was ancient history.

While he was at the institute in Lexington, Jackson found his chief satisfaction in travel and in the fellowship of the Presbyterian Church. Before long he was courting the local preacher's daughter, Ellie Junkin. Jackson had a fondness for dark-eyed brunettes like Ellie. The two were married in 1853. However, Ellie died in the fall of 1854, 14 months after the wedding and during a difficult pregnancy.

Jackson often spent his summer vacations in the North. In 1856, however, he traveled for five months in Europe. By fall, he was back at Virginia Military Institute and pursuing another dark-eyed brunette, Anna Morrison, who was also the daughter of a Presbyterian preacher. Jackson married her the following summer and settled into a sunny domestic routine. But death interceded again when their firstborn, Mary, died of jaundice at three months old.

Now Jackson's health was bothering him, too. Complaining about his hearing and eyesight, he put himself on a diet of plain brown bread, very little meat, and water. He also thought that if he had pepper in his food it would make his left leg ache. And he sucked constantly on lemons. The mysterious ailments grew worse. He put cold-water compresses on his eyes. He even drank poisonous ammonia solutions and chloroform liniment. Nothing seemed to work.

Jackson might have killed himself with his bizarre remedies if it weren't for the troubles between North and South. When Virginia withdrew from the Union in April of 1861, Virginia Military Institute went on a war footing. Four days later, Major Jackson moved the entire student body to Richmond for induction into the Confederate military forces.

Jackson deplored the prospect of war, which he described as the "sum of all evils." Yet if he had any qualms about fighting for the South, he kept them to himself. "I believe God has chosen that my place should be here," was all he said before leaving for Richmond. It was the last Jackson ever saw of Lexington.

Major Jackson was made a colonel in the Virginia forces and took command of Harpers Ferry, the gateway to the Shenandoah Valley. This beautiful valley was the garden spot of Virginia. Threaded by year-round streams and filled with farmland and orchards, it formed an abundant agricultural-supply reserve for the Confederate army.

Training was lax at Harpers Ferry, but it commenced in earnest when Jackson arrived. He quickly whipped 2,100 Virginians and 400 Kentuckians into shape. At first his men did not care for him. Jackson had a strange quality of overlooking human suffering. During one of his battles, Jackson asked the whereabouts of a certain soldier. He was killed, a Virginian infantryman said. "Very commendable," Jackson replied.

Besides working his men too hard, he didn't look as if he could be a leader. He wore a weather-beaten cap and gigantic boots, with the plainest of uniforms, often mud-spattered. He frequently was seen lifting one of his arms to its full length above his head, as if invoking a divine blessing or judgment. Actually the gesture derived from nothing more than his belief that the arm was contracting and needed to be stretched.

Jackson's religious impulses became well-known throughout the army. On the eve of battle, he would rise several times during the night for prayer. And he was so strict an observer of the Sabbath that he would not even write his wife a letter when he thought it would be in transit on Sundays. Yet so many of his battles were fought on Sunday that his men suspected that he preferred to fight on that day because the Lord would be with him. His command, he said, was "an army of the living God as well as of its country."

The Stonewall Brigade got its first marching orders when Union troops were about to cross the Potomac and attack Harpers Ferry. Jackson took off and cut part of the B & O Railroad in Martinsburg. Then he moved his forces out of town and waited for the Yankees to cross the Potomac. When they did, Jackson and his brigade retreated.

Now with the enemy right on his tail, Jackson stopped dead in his tracks. The Union army suddenly jammed behind him for miles. Then he turned and attacked, sending the Yankees scrambling back into Martinsburg. It was Jackson's first chance to test a strategy that worked for him over and over again in the Shenandoah. Know your enemy well, get him to underrate you, then hit him with all you've got.

The North was served notice: Stonewall Jackson was a force to be reckoned with. More important, the Shenandoah Valley was proven to be a bulwark against attacks on the Confederate capital of Richmond. All of this was to Jackson's credit. On July 4, 1861, he was rewarded with a promotion to brigadier general.

There was no time for Jackson to rest on his laurels, however. Two weeks later, his superiors got word that the Union enemy was advancing on Manassas, Virginia, under General Irvin McDowell. Jackson had his brigade up and marching immediately toward Manassas, also known as Bull Run. They occupied Henry House Hill overlooking a blue mass of McDowell's Yankees. The Federal troops were clamoring toward him. He and his forces were about all that stood between the Union army and the Confederate capital of Richmond.

91

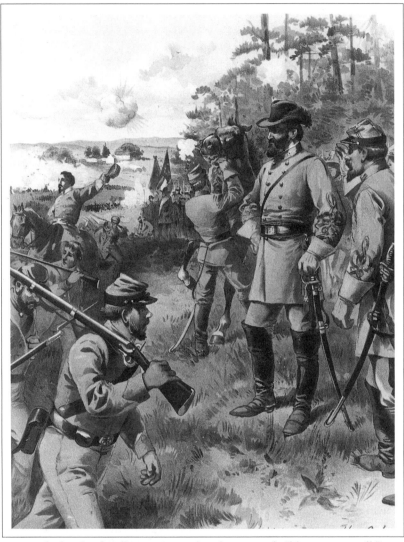

At the battle of Bull Run, General Jackson stands "like a stone wall."
(Library of Congress)

Jackson had a feel for battlefield position. He stuck to his guns and kept them quiet until the enemy forces were within 50 yards. Then he let them have it as they came up the hill. Artillery shells exploded on the advancing Northerners. While other Confederates wavered, Jackson steadfastly withstood the Federal onslaught at a critical moment. It was here that he was given his famous nickname. "Look," one general shouted as his own troops retreated, "there is Jackson standing like a stone wall!" The sobriquet—Stonewall—stayed with Jackson from then on.

The Yankees attacked again in increasing desperation. Stonewall Jackson urged his men to scream like banshees. The "rebel yell" first heard that day would echo from a thousand battlefields. The Union line staggered and fell back, slowly at first, but soon the army was in full retreat. In what became known as the "Great Skeddadle," Union gun carriages became entangled in the buggies of fleeing spectators who had come out from Washington to watch the battle.

The loss, however, did more for the Union than the victory did for the Confederacy. The South, reassured that it could whip the Yankees, still believed the war would be over soon, while the North began to prepare for a long, bloody conflict. Jackson, with his prestige much increased by this battle, became a major general.

In the months immediately succeeding Bull Run, however, he mysteriously disappeared from view, a way he had, as his antagonists were soon to learn. Jackson was almost forgotten, and for a time it seemed that the vital Shenandoah Valley was to know his presence no more.

At the opening of the campaign of 1862, however, Jackson began to loom again upon the military horizon. The fortunes of the Confederacy seemed then at low ebb. But Stonewall Jackson, at least, was delivering strikes in the Blue Ridge Mountains.

In February, Jackson learned that U.S. General Nathaniel Banks had crossed over to Harpers Ferry and was heading for the Shenandoah Valley. Specifically, he was going to Winchester with 40,000 men, under direct orders from President Lincoln to remove the pesky Jackson from the valley.

Jackson's little army had dwindled to barely 3,600 infantrymen by the time Union forces had occupied Winchester. The Yankees outnumbered the Stonewall Brigade ten to one, but Jackson was determined to keep them pinned in the valley. Two days later the brigade reached Kernstown, four miles south of Winchester.

At Kernstown, Jackson's plan to keep the Union forces confined to the valley looked as if it might unravel. The Northerners had tricked him into thinking their massed army was a rearguard action. Still, Jackson refused to retreat. He would never think of retreating. "This army stays here until the last wounded man is removed," he said. "Before I lose them to the enemy, I will lose many more men."

As night fell, Jackson was pushed back with heavy losses, but the Northerners had had enough for one day. Jackson took the opportunity to head south. It was the first and only time he would withdraw from battle. For a time, the fame he had gained after Bull Run was tarnished.

Rumor spread that Jackson was dangerously reckless and that he became insane when excited. It was not until the Shenandoah Valley campaign developed further that the Confederacy realized what a strategic victory he had won: Banks had been kept in the valley instead of going down to Richmond to help Union General McClellan.

At this point, Jackson got the idea that he could turn his infantry into "foot cavalry," an unsaddled force capable of marching nearly as far in a day as a real cavalry force could ride. He began to drill and drill, and seemed always on the march. Jackson's temper flared with stragglers. Deserters could expect to be shot.

Meanwhile, McClellan's Union army had been advancing toward Richmond since April. In May, Jackson started an offensive campaign in the Shenandoah to prevent McClellan from getting additional reinforcements from the Union armies in the valley. Jackson opened the campaign by marching his troops toward the Allegheny Mountains.

On May 8, he attacked Major General John Fremont at the battle of McDowell. The Union was defeated and withdrew to the west. Jackson then marched his troops and, on May 23, overwhelmed a small part of Banks's army at Front Royal, Virginia. When Banks tried to make a break for Winchester, Jackson chased him into town and attacked. Banks's spooked army, which hadn't had a moment to rest, panicked and fled. The Stonewall Brigade captured another 2,500 Yankees and pursued the rest.

The citizens of Washington trembled in fear that Jackson might appear on their streets. President Lincoln, who had had about enough of Jackson, ordered Fremont to attack him from the south. Lincoln also ordered Banks to advance from the north while General McDowell came into the valley from Fredericksburg, to the east. Jackson turned his army south and, with several forced marches, escaped the Union trap, then attacked and defeated these converging armies separately. That ended the valley campaign as Jackson's army boarded trains for Richmond to aid Confederate General Robert E. Lee's army on the Richmond Peninsula.

In just over a month his men had marched almost 400 miles, inflicted 7,000 casualties, and seized huge quantities of badly needed supplies. "He who does not see the hand of God in this is blind," said Jackson. His lightning marches had tied up three separate armies, numbering almost 40,000 troops, which otherwise might have reinforced McClellan on the peninsula. This may have been Jackson's single greatest contribution to the Southern cause.

Now Lee summoned Jackson to Richmond to stop the Union advance on the Confederate capital. But a strange thing happened to Jackson. He seemed to take leave of his senses. He developed a mysterious, debilitating weariness. Instead of moving with the dispatch that he was famous for, he let his army rest. His failure to act quickly was responsible for a bloody Confederate loss along Beaver Dam Creek. It also helped to unravel Lee's elaborate plan to envelop Union General McClellan.

All was not lost, however. Jackson managed to shake off whatever it was that was ailing him. He knew that he had disappointed Lee, a man he had said he would follow into battle anywhere. He desperately wanted to please him. Lee told his prized lieutenant to forget the day's loss. At Cold Harbor, along the Chickahominy River eight miles from the Confederate capital, Lee watched the back of Jackson's grimy gray uniform riding to the battle. Before long, he heard the familiar rebel yell. Jackson was in the midst of his men, sprinting across the fields. Eight thousand Confederates fell, but the Federal line broke, and the Yankees turned tail and retreated.

Jackson marched off to find more Yankees across a bridge over White Oak Swamp. When he arrived there, however, he was so close to physical collapse that his mind was barely functioning. The peculiar weariness had overcome him again. Frozen stiff, he sat out the final portion of the Seven Days' Battle.

Jackson had certainly not lived up to his reputation in the Seven Days' Battle, but he still received good press. In Richmond, he was discomfited to find himself accorded celebrity status. The citizenry flocked around him on the streets. Lee retained full faith in Jackson as well, calling on him to stop yet another threat.

Lee had word that McClellan had been ordered to join Union General John Pope. The tall, bombastic Pope, with his 70,000-strong army, was charging into northern Virginia. Lee and Jackson had decided to divide the army temporarily and to send Jackson by way of Thoroughfare Gap to Manassas Junction, Pope's advance base. Almost at once, Jackson loaded his men's haversacks with three days' rations.

Jackson slipped away on a blitzkrieg march, covering 51 miles in two days. He destroyed two trains, but another two got away. Now the cat was out of the bag. The element of surprise had been blown. Instead of Jackson trapping Pope, Pope was trapping Jackson. Pope's huge army was closing in from both sides like a vise.

Jackson was cornered in the mountains but kept his wits about him. He hid his men in the trees, waiting for Pope's approaching army. As part of it came upon him, the shriek of the rebel yell went out. Jackson's 20,000 men attacked. At the end of the day, Jackson had accomplished his goal. He had attracted Pope's undivided attention. Pope by now had had enough of Jackson and his Stonewall Brigade. The very next day he sent his full army straight at them.

The full might of Pope's army marched up Warrentown Pike and began firing cannon. Vastly outnumbered, the Stonewall Brigade could only muster a thin defense. Then a cry of relief went out among them. A wave of gray columns was moving down on the Yankees from an opposite hill. It was General James Longstreet's 30,000-man wing of Lee's army, which had arrived on the field opposite Pope. The welcome reinforcements rained cannon fire down on the Yankees while Jackson hurled his force at them from the other side. Pope's forces wisely withdrew in full retreat.

Jackson's victory at the battle of Second Bull Run had offset Confederate losses in the West and cleared the way for Lee's invasion of the North. Now Lee moved into Maryland on his first invasion, a Union garrison at the town of Harpers Ferry became a threat to the rear of the Confederate army. Jackson was asked to take Harpers Ferry before meeting Lee across the Potomac.

The town sits astride the confluence of two rivers, beneath three hills to the north, south and west. On the morning of September 15, Jackson was preparing to attack the left flank of the Union line from the west, but the attack became unnecessary when a single Confederate artillery barrage was met with a white flag of surrender.

As Jackson rode into Harpers Ferry, Union troops lined the streets to cheer him. One of the surrendered Union soldiers was heard to say, "Boys, he's not much for looks, but if we'd had him, we wouldn't have been caught in this trap."

The quick victory enabled Jackson to catch up with Lee in Maryland in time to confront McClellan's army with their combined forces. Jackson had his troops up by midnight and marching off in the moonlight. Walking 60 miles in three days, the foot cavalry couldn't recall their last full night's sleep. They were now on Northern soil; and Jackson ordered them into position at Antietam Creek.

What followed for both sides was nothing less than wholesale slaughter, the bloodiest single day of the Civil War. Jackson's battle lines had wavered but held, as thousands of soldiers on both sides fell. He chased the retreating Union troops across a cornfield, only to be repulsed with even heavier losses. When his part of the battle was finally over, Jackson surveyed the dead. Looking out over the field of corpses, he turned to his medical superintendent and said, "God has been very kind to us this day."

That evening, Jackson joined Lee's war counsel and agreed with the others. They were still pinned against Antietam Creek. Good sense dictated that they return to safety. Jackson gave the advice he hated to give—retreat. That night the Southerners built campfires and slipped across the Potomac and back to Virginia.

Tactically, the battle was a draw, but it was a moral, political, and diplomatic victory for the North. Still, Jackson was promoted after Antietam to the rank of lieutenant general.

About the same time, the new commander of the Union's Army of the Potomac had crossed into Virginia. General Ambrose Burnside's plan was to move against Richmond by way of Fredericksburg, in normal times a prosperous town on the Rappahannock River. Burnside's Army of the Potomac made a swift march to Falmouth, a town across the Rappahannock River from Fredericksburg, at a time when the Southern army was widely separated. But due to Burnside's incompetence and a delay in getting pontoon bridges, Lee had time to concentrate his army in the Fredericksburg area.

By December 12 the Union troops had crossed the river, and Burnside started the attack the next morning. The Northerners attacked Jackson but sputtered, giving him enough time to repair his line of defense. Around noon, Burnside attacked a strong Southern position west of the town, where rebel infantry stood behind a stone wall with artillery massed on Marye's Heights above them. The attacks were suicidal as none of Burnside's men got within 20 yards of the stone wall. Darkness finally ended the slaughter. Two days later, under cover of darkness and a heavy rain, the Army of the Potomac recrossed the Rappahannock River. It had been an unmitigated disaster for the Yankees. Another "On to Richmond" drive was stopped. But Jackson was getting more impatient with each invasion.

As spring arrived, he was preparing to meet the enemy again. This time the latest commander of the Army of the Potomac, Joseph Hooker, had come up with another plan to attack Fredericksburg. To stop him, Jackson led his ragged army down through the Wilderness, a seemingly endless forest of scrub brush and timber. Leaving 10,000 of his 37,000 men to hold off the Union left wing, he moved westward into the Wilderness of Spotsylvania to join Lee who was facing the main Union army.

Jackson's foot cavalry marched 20 to 30 miles a day through the thick forest. His men waved their gray caps wildly in the air whenever he rode by. They even prayed with him. Jackson's religious conviction had spread like a fever to his men. Revival tents were set up around camp. Jackson could not have been more pleased with the new religious spirit, but he also knew the importance of his mission. If Hooker turned and attacked, Lee would be crushed.

The fighting began on May 1 when troops led by Jackson challenged Hooker's advance on the Orange Turnpike and Orange Plank Road. Hooker had somehow persuaded himself that Jackson was actually retreating. Unaware of Jackson's presence, the Union troops had been boiling coffee when deer came bounding out of the forest and through their camp. Jackson's army was right behind them. Hooker, who admitted that he "lost his nerve," fell back nearly two miles to a defensive position around Chancellorsville crossroads. Darkness and confusion in the Confederate commands ended Jackson's advance.

Eager to fight on, Jackson rode out between the lines that evening to scout for a night attack. But if the dense woods were good for hiding in, their darkness also made organization impossible. On his way back, nervous Confederate pickets opened fire. Two of Jackson's aides fell dead, shot by their own men. Then another volley. Jackson was hit twice in the left arm. Another bullet hit his right hand.

Jackson was carried to a field hospital. On the way, he was dropped in a fall that shattered his left arm. The arm was removed before gangrene could set in and kill him. Lee was horrified. "He has lost his left arm," Lee said. "I have lost my right."

When Jackson came around from the operation, he seemed to be recuperating. He listened to field reports and gave instructions to his field commanders to force Hooker back. And as the Stonewall Brigade made its last grand charge to victory at Chancellorsville, they cried, "Remember Jackson!" and won the day.

Jackson's high fever kept climbing, however. Then, on Sunday, he took a turn for the worse. Pneumonia was killing him, not the loss of his arm. As he slipped into delirium, Lee continued to worry. The North had been whipped at Chancellorsville. Yet the South had paid sorely for the victory. "Surely General Jackson must recover," Lee said. "God will not take him from us now, not when we need him the most."

In his bedroom, Jackson drifted in and out of consciousness. His surgeon said he would not last the day. "Oh no, my child," Jackson said, when told by his wife. "It's not that serious." Finally, she told him he'd be with the Lord that day. "Good. Very good," Jackson replied. "I always wanted to die on a Sunday."

When they offered him brandy or morphine, Jackson declined, saying he wanted to keep his mind clear. He grew quiet for a spell, then said in a clear, distinct voice: "Let us cross over the river and rest under the shady tree." Then he died.

Today Stonewall Jackson speaks to those who refuse to be defeated against all odds. How he outmaneuvered, escaped from,

"Stonewall" the legendary
(Library of Congress)

and ultimately vanquished three separate armies, each larger than his own, is still a subject of study in military schools. Many critics regard his Shenandoah campaign as the most remarkable display of strategy in all of American military history. Fundamentally, it was based on sound reasoning and the accurate reading of his enemy's plans.

But Jackson was much more than a strategic genius. He was a brilliant inspiration to his men, emerging by surprise from mountain passes and flinging himself upon Union forces with fanatical zeal. It seems that the nickname conferred upon him early in the war was a bit of a misnomer. The "stone wall" had a fabulous mobility.

Civil War historian Shelby Foote says it was Jackson's strange combination of religious fanaticism and glory in battle that made him successful. "He was totally fearless," says Foote, "and he had no thought whatsoever of any danger once a battle was on."

Chronology

January 21, 1824	born in Clarksburg, Virginia
July 1842	enters West Point
June 1846	sent to Mexico
February 29, 1852	resigns from army
July 16, 1857	marries Mary Anna Morrison
June 17, 1861	promoted to brigadier general
July 25, 1861	wins at First Bull Run
October 7, 1861	promoted to major general
May 24–25, 1862	defeats Banks at Winchester
May 31–June 1, 1862	battle of Seven Pines
June 25–July 1, 1862	Seven Days' Battle
August 29–30, 1862	battle of Second Bull Run
September 15, 1862	captures Harpers Ferry
September 17, 1862	battle of Antietam
October 10, 1862	promoted to lieutenant general
December 13, 1862	battle of Fredericksburg
May 1–4, 1863	battle of Chancellorsville
May 10, 1863	dies at Chancellorsville

Further Reading

Bowers, John. *Stonewall Jackson, Portrait of a Soldier*. New York: Avon Books, 1989. An extremely well-written biography of Jackson as a brilliant enigma.

Carpenter, Allan. *Stonewall Jackson: The Eccentric Genius*. Vero Beach: Rourke Publications, 1987. Profiles the personality of Jackson as a Confederate general.

Farwell, Byron. *Stonewall: A Biography of General Thomas J. Jackson*. New York: W. W. Norton, 1992. Solid biography that is very thorough.

Royster, Charles. *The Destructive War*. New York: Knopf, 1991. An interesting examination of Jackson's marches in the Shenandoah Valley.

Philip Henry Sheridan
Fighting Phil

Philip Henry Sheridan as a young soldier
(Library of Congress)

*O*f all the great generals of the Civil War, "Fighting Phil" Sheridan was the purest professional soldier. From the day he entered the military academy at age 18 until the day of his death, he remained in the army. Sheridan disdained all other ambitions, never taking advantage of his prestige as a war hero for political advancement.

When a number of admirers asked him to become a candidate for President, he replied without hesitation, "No man could make me a present of that office. The place-hunters and office-seekers would kill me in thirty days. I could not stand it. I never had any use for politics."

Unquestionably the greatest Union cavalry leader, Sheridan is most famous for his raids near the Confederate capital of Richmond at the end of the war. He is immortalized in verse for his dashing maneuvers around the Confederate army, which contributed to the surrender of the South. Not surprisingly, beloved as he was to the North, he was as hated in the South. For he was the Yankee who laid waste to Virginia's beautiful Shenandoah Valley, the food basket of the Confederacy, reducing its civilians to a state of starvation.

Philip Henry Sheridan was the third of six children of John and Mary Sheridan, who came to America from County Cavan, Ireland, around 1830, after a short period in Canada. On March 6, 1831, Philip Henry Sheridan, their second son, was born, by his own account, in Albany, New York. While Philip was still an infant they moved, in search of opportunity, to the Ohio frontier village of Somerset.

John Sheridan was an industrious man who never hesitated to accept the toughest of work. He settled happily for a living as a laborer upon the canals and roads then under construction. Somerset was located along the most traveled highway from St. Louis to Pittsburgh. A perpetual stream of emigrants making their way westward rolled along its course. Merchants with pack trains loaded with furs and Spanish dollars passed through on their way from remote trading posts.

Philip showed a passionate fondness for horses at a very young age. When he was just five, some older lads, in fun, placed him on a spirited horse found grazing in a nearby field. The animal was spooked somehow. It tossed its head and dashed off, without bit or bridle, at breakneck speed over rails and fences. Phil clung to the horse's mane while the pranksters nervously anticipated his fall. But to their utter consternation, he seemed to be actually enjoying his first riding experience.

Horse and rider vanished, out of sight. Mile after mile the future cavalry leader raced until the horse suddenly turned into a tavern where its owner had been in the habit of stopping. Bystanders hardly knew what to make of the wide-eyed boy on horseback. Villagers gathered to see the remarkable little bareback rider. The tavern filled as more people gathered to hear the story of the young rider repeated. "Who learned you how to ride?" a voice shouted from the crowd. "Nobody," answered the boy. "Did no one teach you how to sit on a horse?" asked another. "Oh, yes. Bill Seymour told me to hold on with my knees, and I did."

The village school, which was conducted in true frontier fashion, provided Phil with the most rudimentary kind of education. Even this was interrupted when he became a clerk in a local dry-goods store at the age of 19. War drums were then beating in Mexico. Phil, however, was too young to follow the youths of Somerset when they enlisted for the Mexican War. This was a bitter disappointment, which was softened only by his appointment to the United States Military Academy.

In 1847, the representative of his district had intimated to Sheridan's father that he would secure an appointment to the Military Academy at West Point if the boy could pass the examination. General Ritchie, who had recently won a seat in Congress, had known Phil as a faithful, energetic, and polite dry-goods clerk.

Young Phil was fired with ambition at the prospect of becoming an army officer. Every night he applied himself, studying before the dim light of the tallow candle in the back part of the store. He passed the written exam, and was barely tall enough to be admitted. In fact, Sheridan made a rather sorry appearance among the proud scions of the wealthy families who were considered the most distinguished people in America. He was still short and slight, barely five and a half feet tall, and somewhat awkward in appearance.

Nor did Sheridan show any remarkable signs of brilliance. He concentrated on his horsemanship and, with the aid of his roommate, succeeded in passing the exams. A pronounced reserve characterized him at all times. But this quiet, retiring manner masked an inner feistiness, as those who were so unsoldierly as to talk down to the little backwoodsman quickly discovered. Sheridan's pugnacious tendencies soon brought him to grief. A scrape with a cadet-officer, who, Sheridan believed, had treated him unjustly, reached a climax when Sheridan pursued his superior with fixed bayonet. Sheridan was suspended from the academy for a year, but subsequently was graduated with the class of 1853, number 34 in a class of 49.

Having finished his military education, Sheridan was commissioned as a second lieutenant in the First Infantry and immediately sent to the Rio Grande frontier in Texas. From that time until the spring of 1855, the young lieutenant saw action against the

Comanches and Apaches, the Indian tribes of the Southwest. In one hairbreadth escape, three soldiers, including Sheridan, were caught by a small party of Apaches just a short distance from the garrison of Fort Duncan.

Thinking quickly, and moving even faster, Sheridan jumped on the bare back of the steed from which the Apache chief had just alighted. Sheridan then made a mad gallop for the fort amid a shower of arrows. Troops quickly followed him back to the rescue of the two scouts left behind.

In 1855, Sheridan was transferred to the 4th Infantry. After a brief service at Fort Wood in New York Harbor, he was sent with a detachment of recruits by way of the Isthmus of Panama to San Francisco. On arriving there, he was immediately ordered to what was then the Washington Territory. At that time the Yakima Indians were on the warpath, and Sheridan was placed in command of a detachment of dragoons, or mounted infantry.

In the Columbia River, where it coursed through canyons of the Cascade range of mountains, was an island from which Indians regularly issued forth to attack the pioneer settlements. Determined to take the island, Sheridan dismounted a company of dragoons. Using a ferryboat, they dropped down the river silently and attacked the island. Sheridan found he was greatly outnumbered, however. His skill in conducting the retreat with the loss of only one man averted what might have been a massacre.

When the Civil War began in 1861, Sheridan was still a captain. Never questioning on which side of the war he would fight, in the spring of 1861, he reported for duty in St. Louis and awaited his Union assignment. To his chagrin, he was ordered to begin his war service as quartermaster and commissary of Union troops. It soon became obvious that his true talents lay in the field. Sheridan's aggressive spirit chafed under the restrictions of staff duties—a dull matter of transporting rations and looking after tents, baggage, and supplies.

He was naturally elated by his appointment as colonel of the 2nd Michigan Cavalry on May 25, 1862. At first his soldiers called their colonel "Little Phil," yet he soon won from them their complete confidence. He was always just and considerate, never asked his men to go anywhere he would not, and was personally at the front of every battle. He also spoke personally and informally to his men, telling them just what he was going to do and when and how he was going to do it.

Sheridan was never a diligent student of military science, but his natural aptitude for command always led him to follow the two cardinal rules he fought by: to take the offensive whenever possible, and to wring the last possible advantages from a defeated enemy. It did not take his cavalry company long to see that it was under the command of a natural.

In short time Sheridan pulled up his force about 20 miles from the Union army at Booneville, Mississippi, a little town in bottom-land country, flanked on one side by an impenetrable swamp. Sheridan wanted only to watch the operations of the enemy and protect the front of the advancing Union army. But on July 1, an attack was made on Sheridan's command by a force of Confederate cavalry numbering from 5,000 to 7,000 men. The whole force under Sheridan did not exceed 800.

Threatened with annihilation, Sheridan sent a team of 90 cavalry sabers out on a desperate ride to the rear of the enemy. Then he instructed this little column to thunder down upon the enemy with such loud cheering that it would appear to be an attack by a whole army. As the 90 screaming riders attacked from the rear, Sheridan led the rest of his forces in a charge along the whole Confederate front. Taken completely by surprise, the huge Confederate force dispersed in every direction.

The victory of Sheridan over a force eight times the size of his own attracted the attention of superior officers right away. In a little over a month, he won the stars of a brigadier general. General Sheridan now enjoyed a nationwide reputation as an outstanding cavalry commander. He was ordered to Louisville, Kentucky, and given command of a division of General Don Carlos Buell's army.

From there Sheridan's division marched with Buell's army to the relief of Nashville in October and November, and he was placed in command of a division of the Army of the Cumberland. In Tennessee, the town of Murfreesboro, with Stones River to the west, had become the center of activity during December 1862. It was there that the Confederate commander, General Braxton Bragg, had positioned his Army of Tennessee to block any attempt by the Union army at Nashville to move into the lower South.

Sheridan spent the better part of the night before the bloody battle of Stones River inspecting his lines and seeing to it that every man was in position. About midnight he went to his quarters in the rear and lay down under the open sky, wrapped in a blanket. During the next two days of battle, he practically saved the army with his stubborn resistance to the Confederate advance.

The weakness of the Union army lay in the fact that the right wing extending toward the west was not properly protected and the extreme right was in danger of being outflanked and surrounded by the enemy. Sheridan, who was in the center, had guessed correctly that the main attack would come near the right. When the right gave way, he sent two of his regiments in, and held Bragg's overwhelming force in check. At that point, the fate of the entire battle was in his hands. The Confederates rushed out of the trees toward the new Union line, but they were met by withering fire and fell back. When the battle was over, the Confederates retreated.

In three days of fighting Sheridan had scarcely slept. He'd been constantly under fire. There was no danger to which his men were exposed that he himself did not share. Now Sheridan met Buell on the field. Pointing to the wreck of his decimated division, he said laconically: "Here are all that are left."

Sheridan was but 33 years old, and already his military genius was recognized and acknowledged by all. His victory at Murfreesboro was the first step in the Union plan for cutting the Confederacy east of the Mississippi River in two. The Northern armies could now aim for Chattanooga, and then the lower South. Sheridan's appointment to major general of volunteers followed by the end of the year.

Nothing of great importance happened during the winter. The terrible battle at Stones River seemed to have been such a shock to both armies that, for nearly a year afterward, both sides in this theater of the war avoided conflict. With the autumn of 1863 approaching, the Union's Army of the Cumberland was put in motion again.

Following its defeat at the bloody battle of Chickamauga, the Union army had retreated to Chattanooga, where it was besieged by Braxton Bragg's Confederates. The enemy had possession of the approaches to the city by land and water. Men and animals were starving. Forage and provisions had to be hauled over a long, circuitous wagon road of 75 miles through the Cumberland Mountains. But Sheridan's men never wanted for provisions. He sent them out from camp to forage for chickens, ducks and turkeys.

For 60 days, from their perch on Lookout Mountain, the Confederates rained shells on the Union camp. When General Grant took command of the Army of the Cumberland, he put Sheridan in charge of all the cavalry units, a corps consisting of three divisions, with about 10,000 men fit for duty.

The battle of Lookout Mountain, or "The Battle Above the Clouds"
(Library of Congress)

With General George Henry Thomas, Sheridan's division pressed to the foot of Missionary Ridge and overwhelmed Confederate entrenchments and rifle-pits. Disobeying orders, he then moved his troops forward to the top of the ridge. Under a withering fire from the artillery lining the summit, his men swept up the heights and over the crest of the ridge in a magnificent charge.

Sheridan pushed on in pursuit of the fleeing enemy. Even after a horse was shot out from under him, he quickly remounted and gave chase. So anxious was he for reinforcements that he ordered two of his regiments to fire into thin air. Sheridan wanted his superiors to believe that the battle was still in progress. Despite the sham battle, no reinforcements arrived.

The loss in Sheridan's division was the greatest in the Army of the Cumberland. But it was also his regiments that first planted their flags atop Missionary Ridge as the Confederates fled down the eastern slope. Despite Sheridan's shenanigans, the victory brought him into favor with Grant, who saw that Sheridan might be one of his most useful lieutenants in the future.

Sheridan was placed in command of the cavalry corps of the entire Army of the Potomac. He had not served in Virginia prior to this time, and the country as well as the rank-and-file of this cavalry was new to him. Immediately he ordered a review of the whole command. He scanned every man and horse. Nothing escaped him.

About the first of May 1864, Grant began the Union campaign against Confederate General Robert E. Lee. His plan was to attack Lee directly, and, if not successful, at least force him to keep changing his position. Sheridan's raid began on the morning of May 9. His riders pushed boldly out toward the west and rode completely around Lee's army. Sweeping down upon Beaver Dam, between the main army of General Lee and Richmond, they captured trains, wrecked about 10 miles of track on three important railroads, severed telegraph wires, and liberated about 400 prisoners.

The next day, at Yellow Tavern, Sheridan came into pitched battle with the Confederate cavalry. In one terrible charge, Jeb Stuart, who was considered the soul of the Confederate cavalry, was killed and his force thoroughly defeated. The loss of Stuart was one of the heaviest blows sustained by the Confederacy.

Sheridan then rode down between the Chickahominy River and Richmond, up to the very outskirts of the Confederate capital, causing great alarm there until he was hemmed in on all sides by the enemy. His astounding escape from this trap was one of the more brilliant exploits in American warfare. Under fire, he constructed a bridge across the Chickahominy River, crossed it, made his escape, and defeated the enemy on the other side.

Soon afterward, he again cut the Virginia Central and the Richmond, Fredericksburg and Potomac railroad, capturing another 500 prisoners before the bloody Union defeat at Cold Harbor. He returned to Grant on the 29th of May. In less than three weeks, he had ridden completely around the Confederate army, defeated its cavalry force, destroyed all rail communication with Lee's army, and prepared the way for the advance of Grant's forces to Petersburg.

One last major "open-field" battle took place at Cold Harbor before the two armies settled into the long siege of Petersburg. The war in the eastern theater now turned to trench warfare as both armies dug in. During the months of May, June, and July, Sheridan was engaged in successive raids against the Confederate lines. But his previous victories had already marked him in Grant's eyes as being fit for far more important duties. Early in August 1864, he was placed in command of the Army of the Shenandoah.

Sheridan's first personal instructions from Grant were to drive the enemy south and to destroy all stores and supplies in the fertile Shenandoah Valley. This beautiful region had been furnishing abundant supplies to the Confederate Army throughout the war. Clearing the enemy out of northern Virginia would relieve Washington of a chronic terror. It might also enable the Union forces to use the Shenandoah again as a base of operations.

Having great confidence in Sheridan, Grant nevertheless acted with caution before giving him the final order to advance. He went down from City Point to Harpers Ferry to meet Sheridan, and told him he must not move until Lee had withdrawn a portion of the Confederate force in the valley.

Sheridan prepared his plans with a caution that would have seemed almost dilatory had he not been ordered to proceed carefully. But on the morning of September 19, he attacked with forceful initiative. Going after Confederate General Jubal Early at the crossing of the Opequan River, he fought all day, then drove Early through Winchester, up the valley, and through the passes of the Blue Ridge Mountains.

For three years the valley had sustained Confederate forces which dealt out defeat after defeat to the Northern armies. The same valley had supported the famous "guerrilla bands," such as Mosby's Men, which had wrought so much damage on Union lines. Now Sheridan had wrenched the valley from them at Winchester in one bold action. For this success, he was promptly made brigadier general.

Under orders from Grant, Sheridan then devastated the valley. He ordered his men to destroy all the crops and the barns, mills, factories, and even farming equipment. Herds of cattle, sheep, and horses were driven out and turned loose. Virtually all the inhabitants of the Shenandoah were reduced to a state of starvation. For this Sheridan was severely censured by Southern sympathizers.

In his eyes, however, it was all a matter of military necessity. He had destroyed the resources that the Army of Northern Virginia had continually used to menace Washington and Pennsylvania. If the destruction seemed wanton, or the suffering uncalled for, at least it might bring an early end to the war. Should the enemy return to the valley, it would find no subsistence from the local citizenry.

The enemy would indeed return, and while Sheridan was absent, one month later. Reinforced by Southern cavalry, Early came back and moved forward with secrecy. Unobserved in the fog and darkness, on October 19, five divisions of Early's army struck the Union camp at Cedar Creek early in the morning, as the soldiers slept. Soon a huge retreat was underway, and the whole Union encampment was all but routed.

At this time, Sheridan had just returned from Washington and was resting at Winchester, 20 miles from the field. Hearing the sound of the battle, he gave rein to his famous black charger "Rienzi," now called "Winchester," after his latest victory. Sheridan rode rapidly and arrived on the field at half past 10. Riding among his troops, he whipped up their fighting spirit.

"Face the other way, boys! We are going back!" Sheridan shouted to the retreating waves of bluecoats. Every group that he met cheered him wildly, turned about and faced the other way. Soon the woods were singing with their minié balls. Sheridan galloped back and forth between the two firing lines to let his whole army know that he was present.

The result at Cedar Creek was astonishing. Sheridan's demoralized troops had regrouped and rallied behind him. He then reformed his lines and launched his counterattack in the afternoon. The enemy was taken completely off guard. Many rebel soldiers had already left their ranks to plunder the fruits of their victory when Sheridan suddenly struck back. Two columns of the Confederate army that were still intact were caught and hurled back. The column on the left crumbled and fled southward in full retreat until they reached Staunton. The rest followed, never to return to the Shenandoah Valley.

The Yankees had lost 13,000 prisoners and given up nearly 17,000 dead or wounded. But a great Union disaster was averted. The Shenandoah Valley was conclusively protected from Confederate occupation. And Sheridan had won another brilliant victory—for the third time in a month.

With his veteran troops, Sheridan soon received the thanks of Congress, especially for the victory at Cedar Creek. The war was not yet over, but already his famous ride to the battlefield was being celebrated in verse by the poet Thomas Buchanan Reed. In Washington for the ensuing victory celebration, Sheridan stood on the balcony of Willard's Hotel, smoking his cigar and lifting his hat to a parade that was over an hour in passing. Flag after flag passed, each emblazoned with the name of one of Sheridan's victorious battles, his riders waving their triumphant sabers in the air as they trotted past their beloved commander.

In early spring Sheridan joined General Grant at Petersburg to take up the final campaign against Richmond. The situation of the Confederate army had become desperate. When it was confronted with the combined armies of Grant and Sheridan, no alternative remained for the Confederates but to retreat. General Robert E. Lee, with his starved Confederate army, evacuated Richmond on April 3, 1865, and began his melancholy march to the west and south.

A bemedaled Sheridan sits for a portrait outside his field tent.
(Library of Congress)

Sheridan was indefatigable in following him. The supplies that General Lee expected from the south were seized by Sheridan's cavalry and destroyed. Wherever the Confederates advanced they were confronted by Sheridan's cavalry. When they made preparations to attack him, Sheridan drew the screen aside and revealed solid masses of Union infantry.

All avenues of escape were cut off. But perhaps of greater strategic importance was Sheridan's concentration of his forces at Five Forks. Grant had planned another assault against Lee's strained defenses. When the Confederates turned and attacked at Five Forks, Sheridan's cavalry stormed over their barricades, capturing flags, cannon, and more than 3,000 prisoners.

Darkness ended the fighting with Sheridan's troops in possession of Five Forks. Lee's dwindling forces headed for Appomattox Station, where much needed supplies were waiting for them. But to the south, the flash and thunder of artillery told the Southerners that Sheridan had reached Appomattox Station first. His cavalry had thrown itself squarely across the Confederate line of retreat.

On Palm Sunday, April 9, Lee briefly attacked Sheridan's Union cavalry. The Southerners easily pushed aside the horsemen, but behind them stood strong formations of bluecoated infantry. Skirmishing continued until an informal truce ended the fighting that morning.

In the afternoon General Grant rode over to Appomattox Courthouse and met General Sheridan in the road. Grant asked the whereabouts of Lee. Sheridan pointed to the house of Wilbur McLean. Grant's staff, including Sheridan, remained in the front yard. In a few minutes Grant sent for them to come in. There in the front room of the McLean house, Sheridan witnessed the surrender of Lee. It was the last scene in the great drama of the Civil War.

Sheridan returned to Richmond and to Washington, where he was ordered by General Grant to proceed at once to Texas to bring rebel General E. Kirby Smith to terms. The grand review of the armies of Grant, Sheridan, and William Tecumseh Sherman was to take place in late May. Sheridan had a great desire to march at the head of his command there. But Grant's order was imperative. With a heavy heart, Sheridan left for Texas with a large force, knowing he would never see his entire army assembled again.

In Texas, Kirby surrendered almost as soon as Sheridan arrived. But Sheridan was in a convenient position to fight another potential enemy. French Emperor Napoleon III was trying to set up the

Hapsburg Archduke Ferdinand Maximilian as emperor of Mexico, contrary to U.S. foreign policy. Sheridan marched American troops to the north bank of the Rio Grande River, displaying his intention to invade Mexico. The demonstration played a large role in forcing the withdrawal of the French army.

Early in 1867, the Reconstruction Acts were passed. It was a cause to which Sheridan was thoroughly, if sternly, devoted, because he believed it would make the divided country whole again. He was made military governor of Louisiana and Texas, with headquarters at New Orleans. The appointment entailed many delicate problems owing to the bitterness engendered by postwar conditions. Sheridan's policies were characterized by severely repressive measures, but he always maintained that he was acting in the interest of the Reconstruction of the South.

Although he was strongly supported by General Grant, the disapproval of President Andrew Johnson eventually brought about Sheridan's transfer to the command of the Department of the Missouri. As he had as a young dragoon, Sheridan was to fight Indians. His mounted infantry rounded up Cheynnes, Comanches, Arapahoes, and Kiowas, forcing them to settle upon Indian reservations.

As President in 1869, Grant made Sheridan a lieutenant general. The following year Sheridan went abroad, during the Franco-Prussian War, to visit the German armies in the field. After a year's absence, he returned to assume command of his military division, with headquarters in Chicago.

There Sheridan married Irene Rucker, the daughter of the quartermaster general of the army. Two years later he was again sent to the city of New Orleans, to quell political rioting. He was placed in command of the western and southwestern military divisions in 1878. Six years later, he succeeded General Sherman as commander-in-chief of the U.S. Army.

On June 1, 1888, Congress bestowed upon him the highest military rank, that of full general. The last months of his life were occupied by the writing of his *Personal Memoirs*, the preface being signed only three days before his death on August 5 at Buzzards Bay, Massachusetts, where he had gone with his family in the hope of restoring his failing heart.

Sheridan's funeral, with imposing military and civil honors, took place in Washington, D.C., and he was laid to rest in the National Cemetery at Arlington among 16,000 of his comrades.

He was survived by his widow and by four children—three daughters and a son.

It should be noted that Sheridan rose to his conspicuous military position only near the end of the war. And his greatest successes were won from a numerically inferior and poorly mounted foe. But historians agree that Sheridan was one of the greatest of all cavalry leaders. For one thing, he could adapt to circumstances and modify plans instantly in battle. His orders were as swift as lightning. For another, he was personally in the forefront of every battle in which his command was engaged, imparting his enthusiasm to every man serving under him.

His actual personal influence over his men was perhaps as great as any general's, including Lee. He could rouse his men to a fever pitch of enthusiasm. It is also worth noting that perhaps nowhere in the history of the world has a routed army ever returned to the field on the day of its defeat and snatched a victory. Philip Henry Sheridan did this at Cedar Creek, without reinforcements!

"When the battle waged hottest, Sheridan was at his best—cool, exact, self-possessed, the dashing and brilliant leader of men willing to follow him anywhere," says historian Phineas Headley. "His order of battle was formed swift as the wrath of the summer storm. There was no delay, no hesitation, no argument—the moment he saw the enemy he was ready for action."

Chronology

March 6, 1831	born in Albany, New York
July 1853	graduated from West Point
November 22, 1854	made 2nd lieutenant
March 1, 1861	promoted to captain
May 25, 1862	promoted to colonel
December 31, 1862	battle of Stones River
November 23–25, 1863	battle of Missionary Ridge
May 5–6, 1864	commands cavalry of Army of the Potomac; battle of the Wilderness
May 10, 1864	battle of Beaver Dam
August 1864	commands Army of the Shenandoah
September 19, 1864	defeats Jubal Early at Winchester
October 19, 1864	defeats Jubal Early at Cedar Creek
November 8, 1864	promoted to major general
April 1, 1865	forced Confederate retreat at Petersburg
April 9, 1865	engages Lee at Appomattox Station
1867	military governor of Texas and Louisiana
March 1869	made lieutenant general
1873	selected to command American forces
June 3, 1875	marries Irene Rucker
1878	in command of West, Southwest Divisions
1883	becomes commander-in-chief of army
1888	made general-in-chief
August 5, 1888	dies in Buzzards Bay, Massachusetts

Further Reading

Hutton, Paul Andrew. *Phil Sheridan and His Army*. Lincoln: University of Nebraska Press, 1985. A in-depth look at Sheridan's military feats.

Reeder, Russell Potter. *Sheridan, the General Who Wasn't Afraid to Take a Chance*. New York: Duell, Sloan and Pearce, 1962. An examination of Sheridan's character and his daring as a cavalry leader.

Sheridan, Philip Henry. *Personal Memoirs of P. H. Sheridan, General, U.S. Army*. St. Clair Shores, Mich.: Scholarly Press, 1977. Sheridan's personal account of his service in the U.S. Army.

Jeb Stuart
The Joyous Cavalier

Jeb Stuart
(Library of Congress)

*I*t is not easy to separate Jeb Stuart the soldier from Jeb Stuart the legend. Unquestionably the greatest cavalry leader on either side of the Civil War, he was a picturesque symbol of the proudly romantic South, and looked every bit the part. Stuart liked to ride hard in to battle singing, and always on a splendid horse. He rode so hard, in fact, that no animal could long survive his galloping. Beloved and celebrated though he was, he did have his Southern detractors. They accused him of parading himself for admiration. Stuart indeed did little to discourage the adulation, but he was as ready for a fight as a frolic.

His daring "Ride Around McClellan" immortalized him in Southern legend and military history. It was a pounding, three-day swing around the huge Union Army of the Potomac, with Stuart slowing only to accept bouquets and kisses from admiring Southern women. Stuart laid bare a Northern plan to capture Richmond, and introduced cavalry raiding to the war. Thus, Jeb Stuart managed to be a big showoff and an outstanding cavalry leader at the same time—until struck dead by a Northern bullet at the early age of 31.

James Ewell Brown Stuart, whose initials in later years gave him his famous nickname "Jeb," was born on February 6, 1833, at Laurel Hill plantation in Patrick County, Virginia. The seventh of 11 children, and the youngest son, his ancestors were of Scot-Irish stock on his father's side and Welsh on his mother's.

Both sides of the family had records of public service. His father, Archibald, represented Patrick County in the Virginia Assembly for many years and also was a member of Congress for a time. Besides being a noted orator, Archibald was well-known for his social grace, his wit and great charm. His dash and gaiety obviously rubbed off on Jeb. Archibald was noted for his singing voice, while the qualities of Jeb's voice were soon to become famous.

Jeb also displayed a strong moral fiber that must have been inherited from his mother, Elizabeth Pannil Letcher. She instilled in him an overwhelming devotion to duty, sometimes bordering on piety. It was she who gave Jeb the firm and simple religious training that was always an important force in his life. When he was just 12, she asked him to swear he would never touch liquor. He never did, refusing it even to ease the suffering of the wound that killed him.

From early boyhood Jeb showed all the gritty determination of a fine soldier. An older brother tells of an encounter the two boys had with some hornets when Jeb was nine. They had spotted an unusually large hornets' nest in the branches of a big tree. They shimmied up the tree, closer and closer, when out swarmed the stingers. Jeb's brother dropped to the ground, while Jeb kept at it. Possessed by challenge, and aggressive by nature, he tested his courage. Countless stings could not stop him. Finally he poked a stick at the nest, and down it went.

Jeb was for the most part tutored at home until, at age 15, he entered Emory and Henry College in Virginia. Latin was his favorite subject. He considered it an important part of the preparation for his future career in schoolteaching. His plan to teach was apparently changed quite suddenly. When his father lost his seat in Congress, the opposing candidate's first official act was to appoint Jeb to the United States Military Academy at West Point, New York.

Jeb was 17 years old when he became a West Point cadet. The commandant of the military academy was Lieutenant Colonel Robert E. Lee, who, as general of the Army of Northern Virginia, would later command Jeb in the hostilities that were just beginning to simmer. The sectional problems among the states stirred constant debate among cadets from North and South. Jeb could give as good as he got. Even in those days, when a gentleman fought for his honor at what we today would consider the drop of a hat, Jeb was in more scrapes than most of his fellows.

At the academy he was called "Beauty," though only because they thought he was anything but beautiful. However handsome Jeb afterwards grew, when he would sport his soldierly red beard, as a cadet he was not especially attractive. Still he was popular and was distinguished for his quiet, wholesome religion and, paradoxically, for his "almost thankful acceptance" of almost every challenge to fight, even though he was often beaten. Jeb took his share of demerits for fighting and horseplay, but stood fairly high in his class academically.

Jeb enjoyed his years at West Point, though he missed his home. He said once, "If it could be grafted on Virginia soil I would consider it a paradise." Curiously, his rank dropped sharply during his last two years. It is said that he deliberately let his grades slide. It seems that the cadets with the highest grades automatically went into the Corps of Engineers. Stuart preferred the cavalry, and so, they say, he let his class standing fall just low enough to disqualify him for the Engineers.

Stuart finished 13th in the class of 46 who survived. Assured of a cavalry unit, his first assignment was in Texas with the mounted rifles, infantrymen who used their horses merely for transportation, not combat. There, out of Fort Clark, Stuart patrolled territories inhabited by Apache and Comanche Indians. It was some of the toughest terrain in the world, covering the Trans-Pecos and

Texas Panhandle, and always subject to brief encounters with Indians. Stuart's expeditions did not go unnoticed. In the spring of 1855 he was chosen as one of the officers for the proud new 1st Cavalry Regiment.

It was an elite corps that was being created for quick-moving scouts in Kansas. There, too, Indian troubles were brewing among the Cheyennes. But life at Fort Leavenworth wasn't all that appealing. Stuart's first assignment, as regimental quartermaster, was decidedly unglamorous, but it gave him firsthand experience with all the problems of keeping a modern cavalry fed, supplied, and mounted.

And he quickly found a pleasing diversion on the lonely plains of Kansas. Colonel Philip St. George Cooke, a fellow Virginian and the commandant at Fort Leavenworth, had three daughters. One of them, Flora, caught Stuart's eye as soon as he arrived. He wooed and won her in a whirlwind courtship that had them engaged within three weeks of his joining the regiment. He then left for an expedition against the Indians. By the following fall he returned and they were married.

Flora was a skilled horsewoman, and she and Jeb shared many rides along the paths near Fort Leavenworth when he wasn't off fighting Indians. But they were often separated during the early years of their marriage. Bloody conflict was shaking Kansas over its future as a slave state or free state. Stuart was kept busy trying to keep the peace among abolitionists and pro-slavery factions, as well as Indians.

In one raid by about 300 Cheyennes, Stuart was shot while saving the life of a fellow officer who had run out of bullets. The bullet glanced to the left of Stuart's heart as it entered his chest. Otherwise, he might have been killed. For his bravery he was promoted to the rank of first lieutenant.

In 1859 Stuart came back East, chiefly in the hope of selling to the War Department the rights to a device he had invented for attaching the cavalry saber to a soldier's belt. While in Washington in October, he was asked to ride in haste to Arlington with a sealed message for Robert E. Lee, his old commandant at West Point. Lee had been ordered to command the marines being sent to Harpers Ferry, about 50 miles away, to put down a slave insurrection by militant abolitionists.

Stuart was accepted as Lee's aide-de-camp and went with him to Harpers Ferry. There, at an arsenal where the abolitionists were barricaded, Stuart was sent to read a surrender demand to the leader of the uprising. It was John Brown, whom Stuart recognized as the same John Brown who had gained famed as an abolitionist while Stuart was in Kansas.

As Brown listened to Stuart's order, he held the door open a crack and a cocked carbine ready to fire. Brown later said, "I might have killed him, just as easy as I could kill a mosquito." When Brown refused to surrender, Stuart stepped back and waved his cap in the air. At this signal, the marines stormed the arsenal. Brown was captured, and Stuart had helped to make history.

Back on the frontier, Stuart was promoted to captain. The new stripes hardly seemed to matter though. Differences between the Northern and Southern states were quickly coming to a head. In March, Stuart obtained a two-month leave and waited anxiously for news of his native state. When news came that Virginia had seceded, Stuart wrote Jefferson Davis and asked for a position in the Confederate army. He then started out for his native state. En route he mailed in his resignation from the United States Army.

At home in Virginia, Stuart found that secession had split his family. Flora's father, Colonel Cooke, remained loyal to the Union, a decision Stuart said Cooke would "regret but once, and that would be continuously." A brother-in-law went North, too, while a second brother-in-law stayed in the South. Stuart, meanwhile, was commissioned as a lieutenant colonel of the Virginia infantry.

His first orders were to report to Colonel Thomas "Stonewall" Jackson in Virginia's Shenandoah Valley. The two could not have been more different in appearance or nature. Stuart was full of song and laughter; Jackson was quiet and solemn, almost to the point of rudeness, and rumpled and careless in dress. Stuart was impeccably dressed, and had finally grown into a very handsome man, his big red beard, tinged blond in the sun, adding to his soldierly appearance. But the two soldiers were to become fast friends. Both were religious men. And both were fighters.

Within two weeks Jackson had made Stuart a captain of the 1st Virginia Cavalry. Stuart was almost never found in camp. His cavalrymen soon found that he rewarded them by giving them hazardous duty. It was the sort of thing he liked best. Stuart assumed it was what they would like best as well.

At First Manassas, or Bull Run, with a well-timed charge Stuart and his cavalry helped to save the day when things looked darkest for the Southern troops. It was July 21, and Stuart's cavalry had rode 60 miles in two days. Stuart's job was to cover Stonewall Jackson's left flank.

At one point, when the battlefield was covered in thick artillery smoke, Stuart spurred his horse forward and led about 300 cavalrymen straight into enemy fire. The force of his drive helped to scatter the Yankees. Stuart and his yelling cavalry swept down upon the rear of the retreating Union army, completing its rout and with Stuart leading the pursuit.

In September, he was rewarded for the Southern victory with a commission of brigadier general of cavalry. During the next few months, Stuart's wife and their two toddlers—young Flora and Jemmie—were frequent visitors to Jeb's headquarters. Jeb and Flora were often entertained at the surrounding plantations. On such evenings there was bound to be music, and always singing when Jeb was around. Flora had a pleasant voice as well, and played guitar. Jeb loved to dance. Even in his camp there was singing and dancing, but never any drinking or swearing in his presence.

Off duty, Stuart was gay and boisterous, seemingly boyish and carefree. Accompanied by a banjo player whenever possible, he and his column would often break into song with his old favorite, "Jine the Cavalry." He was always a dashing figure. His gray cloak was lined with red, and a red flower or red-ribboned love-knot decorated its lapel. His hat was cocked on one side, a peacock's plume fastened to it by a gilded star, and his long, flowing beard gleamed in the sun.

The largest engagement of this period was the battle of Dranesville. Though surprised and nearly mauled by a Union force nearly twice the size of his, Stuart and his 2,400 men fought stubbornly in order to buy time for the larger Southern army to move its wagon trains into safe position for a withdrawal. Despite the defeat, his men emerged with even more confidence in their young general because of the skill he had shown in getting them out of a dangerous situation.

Soon Stuart was to become a frequent visitor at the tent of General Lee, now commander of the Army of Northern Virginia. Lee wished to know whether McClellan held the watershed between the Chickahominy and Potopotomoy rivers, down which he intended to bring Jackson's Army of the Shenandoah. He also asked Stuart to destroy McClellan's wagon trains. If the maneuver were successful, the whole Union army might be rendered vulnerable.

The next day, with 1,200 cavalry and a section of artillery, Stuart set out. Thus began the Chickahominy Raid, also known as Stuart's famous "Ride Around McClellan." He reconnoitered the

Union forces and led his troops on a pounding, three-day, 350-mile ride around McClellan's huge army. His men burned Federal camps, cut down telegraph poles, took prisoners, horses and mules, and slowed down only to accept the bouquets and kisses of admiring Southern belles. In vain pursuit was Stuart's father-in-law, Philip Cooke, now a general in the Union army.

Stuart ascertained that McClellan's right did not extend to the watershed. He might then have turned back but decided the safest course was to make a complete circuit around the Union Army of the Potomac. He kept his horses galloping for days. His sleepy horsemen stole naps while still in the saddle. Stuart himself rode ahead to Richmond, galloping for some 48 hours straight to reach General Lee with the news that was to prove of great value.

Time and again Lee relied on Stuart for such intelligence. And it always proved to be accurate and valuable. No wonder Lee was to say of Stuart, with the highest praise: "He never brought me a piece of false information." Lee regarded Stuart almost as a son and remarked after the war that Stuart was his ideal of a soldier.

Now Stuart was able to carry out the second part of Lee's instructions: to destroy any enemy supplies he came across. He rode out and wrecked still more large transports carrying supplies. A wagon train, railroad cars, other rolling stock, and a railroad bridge were all destroyed by Stuart in the final phase of the campaign that drove McClellan from the peninsula. Richmond was kept safe from a Northern invasion.

A period of relative calm for both the Confederate and Union armies followed this campaign. Flora and the two children were able to join Stuart again, but the peaceful interlude could not last. In August, Major General John Pope was concentrating another Union army at Manassas Junction.

Under Lee's order, Stuart rode clear around the rear of the Union army, crept in close under cover of darkness, and sprang his trap on the enemy's headquarters by the Rappahannock River. The Yankees scattered, and the rebels took over quickly. Taking stock of the confiscated loot, Stuart found that it included the personal baggage of Union General John Pope, a man as hated in the South as any living Northerner.

Stuart laughed with glee. The cache contained detailed information on Pope's plans. The information led Lee to decide that the time to act was now. Pope should be attacked before he received reinforcements. Accordingly, Stuart and his cavalry, with two regiments of Stonewall Jackson's feared infantry, rushed toward Manassas Junction, the huge Federal depot that was a critical connection in the Union army's lifeline to Washington. The station was taken before the Northern forces could succeed in burning it to keep the supplies from falling into Confederate hands. A feast day followed as the hungry rebels gorged themselves on pickled oysters, potted lobsters, and slabs of cheese. Stuart covered the infantry's flanks as they marched off, whole hams skewered on the blades of their bayonets.

Stuart waited nearby for Longstreet's 30,000-man wing of the Army of Northern Virginia while keeping an eye on the advancing Union army. Knowing that the Northerners far outnumbered Jackson's column, Stuart attempted a ruse. On a thickly forested ridge, he set his men to work cutting down pine branches. Dragging the branches behind them, the riders kicked up such a cloud of dust that the oncoming Yankees thought they were in the presence of Lee's entire army. As a result, the blue Union troopers were very slow and cautious in moving. When they did move, the next day, the rest of Lee's army had indeed arrived to help Jackson, and blasted big gaps in their lines. That night, Pope began his withdrawal from Manassas.

Until now, Stuart had spent all of his time on his home turf in Virginia. Now General Lee had decided to bring the war to the North. In the fall of 1862, Stuart set out across the Potomac with 1,800 men and four guns to make a raid into Union territory.

Once again, Lee split his army. Militarily, it fell to Stuart and the cavalry to open the mountain passes between the captured Harpers Ferry and the main Confederate army until Jackson could rejoin Lee in Maryland. Stuart fell in behind Jackson, with Yankees nipping at his heels the whole way. Finally the two huge armies of the Union and the Confederacy faced off in Sharpsburg, Maryland, along a creek called Antietam.

What followed was the war's fiercest fighting yet. As the bullets flew overhead, Stuart rode across the battlefield directing his men. The battle of Antietam, the war's bloodiest day so far, closed with the Confederate line intact. The next evening, when the expected Union attack did not materialize, Lee decided to retreat. Southern plans for a northern invasion had fallen short of success.

As the days went by, General Lee decided to probe the Union forces again in Maryland. It was October, and Stuart would thumb his nose at McClellan one more time before settling into winter headquarters. For the second time in his career, Stuart rode around McClellan's entire Army of the Potomac. He crossed the

Potomac River again, but was unable to destroy an iron railroad bridge at Chambersburg, Maryland, and had to turn back. Before he did, however, he captured a large number of horses, while losing only two of his own men. Stuart also returned with 30 prominent citizens as hostages for Virginia citizens the United States had seized.

The raid was not successful in carrying out Stuart's main objective, but it did underscore Northern military futility. In November, President Abraham Lincoln replaced McClellan, who had failed to produce a clear-cut Union victory. Even after McClellan had turned back the Confederate invasion at Antietam, his failure to follow up with a blow to the retreating rebels had disappointed Lincoln.

Stuart quickly discovered that General Ambrose Burnside, the new commander of the Army of the Potomac, was settling in along the Rappahannock River. Everyone knew that for now the safety of the whole Army of Northern Virginia would depend on the continued watchfulness of the cavalry. Stuart was kept busy guarding the Rappahannock fords and making raids to the rear of Burnside's army.

On one such expedition, Stuart rode in and surprised a Union telegraph operator at Dumfries Station. Always fond of a joke, he had his own operator send a message to the Union quartermaster general in Washington: "I am much dissatisfied with the transport of the mules lately sent which I have taken possession of, and request that you send me a new supply."

Burnside was soon relieved of his command of the Army of the Potomac. In the spring of 1863, his replacement, Major General Joseph Hooker, threatened to cross the Rappahannock River as Burnside had earlier. Stuart gave Lee prompt word of Hooker's movement across the river. He also sent word to Lee that he had found an old, little-used wagon road circling around Hooker's army.

On the basis of this information, Lee decided to send Stonewall Jackson down this road to pounce upon Hooker's rear the next day. Stuart helped protect Jackson's march, and held a road to the main battlefield where Lee would attack. When Jackson was mortally wounded by an accidental shell from one of his own men, Stuart was summoned to take command of Jackson's II Corps.

Stuart worked the rest of the night acquainting himself with the terrain and the disposition of the Federal troops. A scouting report showed that the key enemy position was Hazel Grove, a ridge on which the Union artillery was posted in strength. It was there that

Stuart chose to attack with Jackson's men the next day, without regard for losses.

The fighting was furious at dawn. Artillery brigades from various Confederate divisions united to attack Hazel Grove. After its capture, Stuart led two charges into the clearing beyond the ridge, his golden voice ringing in the air as he rode into battle brandishing his French saber. The sight of this singing cavalier galloping into the fray created a great surge of enthusiasm among Jackson's troops, whose morale had fallen upon hearing the news of their leader's wound.

Stuart didn't stop to catch his breath until he had crashed through everything. The Confederate forces stood united around a burning manor at Chancellorsville. The entire Union army was turned back across the Rappahannock. Yet when Jackson died a short time later, Stuart was passed over as his successor. The decision had nothing to do with Stuart's qualifications. The absence in the historical record of even a hint that Lee considered Stuart as Jackson's permanent successor is considered evidence that he regarded Stuart as the indispensable head of the cavalry corps.

After the Confederate victory at Chancellorsville, Stuart's cavalry had a short period of rest. His men held balls and a troop review for the edification of the local gentry. During one such ball, word reached him that Union cavalry riders were pouring across the Rappahannock River at nearby Brandy Station.

It was one of the few times in his career that Stuart had been taken by surprise. Twelve hours of charges and countercharges swept back and forth over thousands of acres of ground. At dusk, hearing of the approach of Confederate infantry, the Union cavalry broke off and returned across the Rappahannock. The battle of Brandy Station ended what was without doubt the largest cavalry battle ever to take place in North America.

It had been a hard-fought and costly battle, however, and Stuart was harshly criticized for his negligence in spite of his narrow escape. In the Southern press, it was said that he would not have been taken by surprise had he not spent so much time holding fancy riding exhibits before the ladies and dancing half the night. Brandy Station also proved that the Union cavalry was finally on an equal footing with the main cavalry force of the Confederates.

Now Stuart was given the hard and thankless task of guarding the Blue Ridge Mountain passes until the Confederate infantry passed by. General Lee was moving his army northward toward Pennsylvania. His strategy called for Stuart to play his usual role in protecting the army's advance and in collecting information and provisions.

Stuart learned that Union army, now under General George Meade, was spread out. He thus proposed that he interpose his cavalry between the enemy army and Washington to obtain accurate intelligence of the enemy's movements. Then he would cross the river into Pennsylvania, make contact with a Confederate column of advance units, and report back to Lee. It was an opportunity for Stuart to launch another spectacular raid into enemy territory. Lee assented, but under conditions that he thought would give ample guarantee of Stuart's early return.

Stuart was delayed, however, by the presence of heavy Union columns. An entire wagon train being sent to supply the Northern Army of the Potomac was captured. At the time it seemed a real prize, but the heavy wagons slowed the march of Stuart's cavalry. Constant delays occurred as one wagon driver after another fell asleep from sheer exhaustion.

Lee was now worrying about the absence of Stuart with information about the whereabouts of the enemy. In fact, Lee did not get word from Stuart until three days after he had already learned that the Army of the Potomac was north of its namesake river. He was shocked at the proximity of the concentrated enemy while his own forces remained scattered.

Meanwhile, Stuart's exhausted force crawled along at an unbearably slow pace. When he finally reached Gettysburg, Lee was already battling Meade in the second day of fighting. It had been eight days since Lee had seen Stuart. "Well, General, you are here at last," were Lee's only words to Stuart when he finally arrived. Stuart appeared genuinely shaken by the comment, although he tried not to show it at the time. But it was not the absence of cavalry as a fighting force that Lee had regretted, for he had two of Stuart's brigades with him at all times. It was the absence of Stuart himself that nagged him. Lee had come to rely on Stuart personally.

That day the Confederate infantry was torn to shreds when Pickett's famous charge up Cemetery Hill was gunned down by artillery fire at a terrible loss to the Southern forces. Lee and his damaged army slipped safely back to Virginia soil, but the defeat at Gettysburg was partly blamed on Stuart's absence. In his report, Stuart claimed that he had performed a larger service than he could have rendered had he remained with the main army. Many others asserted then—and still do today—that Stuart had deprived

"Pickett's Charge," at the battle of Gettysburg
(National Archives)

his chief of victory by riding off on a bootless raid that kept Lee and all his senior lieutenants groping in the dark.

Whatever the case, never again could Stuart be accused of failing to keep the commanding general informed of hostile movements. In October, in a lesser engagement, Lee asked him to reconnoiter the Union forces in the vicinity of Catlett's Station, on the Orange and Alexandria Railroad. Stuart set out at once. Coming suddenly out of the woods, he found himself at a vantage point he could hardly believe. Spread out below him in blue columns along the railroad tracks was what appeared to be the whole of the Union Army of the Potomac.

Stuart did not have the forces needed to confront such a large army, but he ordered the cannons loaded and quietly rolled them forward anyway. Then he gave the order. "Fire!" he shouted. Confederate cavalrymen fired cannons with the skill of infantrymen. Stuart waved his saber and down raced his troopers, guns and wagons rattling behind them. Around the Union flank they galloped furiously. All it would take to get back to the shelter of Lee's army was a routine ride. Instead, Stuart let the enemy follow, then suddenly turned and attacked. The Union troops wheeled around in confusion and raced off. For five miles the Confederate cavalry galloped after them. Ever after, they referred to the engagement as the "Buckland Races."

The hard riding of the battles of 1863 had almost decimated the cavalry corps of the Army of Northern Virginia. Stuart's men lacked food and clothing. A dwindling number of horses endured almost constant hunger and thirst. With the approach of spring in 1864, it was plain that the cavalry could not undertake long operations on the meager forage the Confederate quartermaster could provide. Starvation seemed an ominous possibility.

In early May, the Union forces crossed the Rapidan River with a new commanding general who had achieved an impressive series of victories in the western theater: Ulysses S. Grant. Stuart, for a few days, was able to cover Lee's operation and to supply indispensable information concerning Northern troop movements. Summoning all the men he could muster—about 4,500— Stuart demanded of the weak horses their last mile of endurance.

Union General Philip Sheridan, who had been called up from the Shenandoah Valley, led a large force of artillery and about 10,000 cavalry on a wide detour, then headed straight south, and, with no deception, challenged Stuart's fabled troopers to attack. They chased Sheridan's horsemen, nipping at his heels but failing to prevent the destruction of twenty miles of railroad and an extremely valuable supply of rations for Lee's army.

In a cruel clash at Yellow Tavern, only 60 miles from Richmond, Stuart pushed Sheridan's columns off the road to the Confederate capitol. But outnumbering the rebels two to one and outgunning them with rapid-fire carbines, the blue troopers came back and rolled over Stuart's once-invincible cavalry. It was his last stand.

The plumed cavalier, who had not been touched by a bullet or saber in all his battles for the Confederacy, was wounded at close range by a dismounted Union cavalryman. He died the next day, May 12, in a blow to the Confederate leadership that hurt almost as much as the death of Jackson a year and a day earlier, and perhaps even more because it came at a time when Lee's army was disappearing.

The defeat of the Confederacy seemed to be only a matter of time when Stuart was buried in Richmond, a man honored and loved among his fellow men-at-arms and compatriots in a way that few soldiers have ever been. Historians still argue about his value as a military commander. As a cavalry commander, all

The burning and evacuation of Richmond—April 3, 1865
(Library of Congress)

agree, he was flawless in the execution of Lee's first invasion of the North. His daring run around McClellan's army in 1862 not only introduced cavalry-raiding to the war but also boosted Confederate morale when the war seemed to be going badly.

But some have questioned Stuart's military skills. Why he slipped the leash and went off on his wild and irrelevant raid before Gettysburg will always remain a controversial question. No one can say for sure whether Stuart's arrival two days earlier would have made a difference. The evidence simply doesn't permit a definite conclusion. Suffice it say that Lee's orders to Stuart, though somewhat vague, obligated Stuart to abandon any undertaking that would delay him. Stuart encountered hindrances, but, characteristically, pressed on anyway in his stubborn adventure.

What can be said with certainty about Stuart is that he was by far the greatest cavalry leader of the war. In the words of historian Emory M. Thomas, "Stuart displayed the capacity to command both small and large numbers of horsemen, and he was able to integrate his cavalry with artillery and infantry, as well as conduct independent operations." Other cavalry leaders proved they could do some of these things, adds Thomas. "But Stuart did them all and did them consistently well."

Chronology

February 6, 1833	born in Patrick County, Virginia
1850	graduates from Emory and Henry College
July 1, 1854	graduates from West Point
1855	transfers to 1st U.S. Cavalry
November 14, 1855	marries Flora Cooke
December 29, 1855	promoted to 1st lieutenant
April 22, 1861	made captain in U.S. Army
May 3, 1861	resigns from army after promotion to captain
May 10, 1861	commissioned lt. colonel of Virginia Infantry
May 24, 1861	made captain of Confederate cavalry
July 21, 1861	battle of First Manassas
September 21, 1861	promoted to brigadier general
June 1, 1862	begins first ride around McClellan
July 1, 1862	Seven Days' Battle
July 21, 1862	promoted to major general
October 9, 1862	begins second ride around McClellan
June 9, 1863	battle at Brandy Station
May 12, 1864	dies in battle at Yellow Tavern

Further Reading

Davis, Burke. *Jeb Stuart, The Last Cavalier*. New York: Fairfax Press, 1988. A well-written look at Stuart as a symbol of the proud Old South.

de Grummond, Lena Y., and Lynn de Grummond Delaune. *Jeb Stuart*. Philadelphia: Lippincott, 1962. A lively biography for young readers.

Thomas, Emory M. *Bold Dragoon*. New York: Harper & Row, 1988. A comprehensive if flatly written critical biography of Stuart.

Index

Bold numbers indicate main headings

Index

Index

stand of 13; Longstreet and 70–71, 76; in Mexican War 5; in Seven Days' Battle 8; in Shenandoah campaign 7; Sheridan raids as setbacks to 110; Stuart and 121, 122, 124; West Point headed by 5; West Point training of 3–4
Lee's Lieutenants (book) 83
Letcher, Elizabeth Pannil 120
Lincoln, Abraham iv; Antietam outcome and 11, 127; assassination of 65; Grant and 13, 54, 59; Kentucky politics as problem for 41; Shenandoah campaign and 93–94; Thomas dispute with 28, 31; Union war needs underestimated by 40; Vicksburg siege supported by 61
Longstreet, Augustus Baldwin 71
Longstreet, James vi, *70*, **70–85**, *82*; Advanced Forces commanded by 74; at Antietam 78–79; at Bull Run (1861) 9, 74; at Bull Run (1862) 76–77, 96; chronology 84; early life of 71; at Fredericksburg 79; at Gettysburg 70–71, 80–81; Grant and 72; historians on 83; in Mexican War 72–73; Republican Party joined by 82; in Seven Days' Battle 75–76; at Seven Pines 75; Stuart and 126; Suffolk Campaign of 80; West Point training of 71–72; in Wilderness battle 81
Lookout Mountain, battle of 29–30, *109*
Louisiana 40, 56, 115
Louisiana State University 39

M

Madison, Dolly 87
Magruder, John 88
Malvern Hill 8
Manassas, first battle of *See* Bull Run, first battle of
Manassas, second battle of *See* Bull Run, second battle of
"Manifest Destiny" 56
Maryland 61, 77, 96
Mason, John Young 22
McClellan, George B. v, 76; at Antietam 9–11; Grant contrasted with 13; Jackson failure versus 95; Jackson success versus 94; in Seven Days' Battle 8; at Seven Pines 74–75; Stuart's ride around 120, 124–125, 132
McDowell, battle of 94
McDowell, Irvin 91
McFeely, William 67
McLean, Wilmer 14, 114
McPherson, James M. 16, 50
Meade, George B. 12, 129
Memphis, Tennessee 43
Mexican War (1846) iv, 65; Grant in 56–57; Jackson in 88; Lee in 5; Longstreet in 72; Sheridan in 105; Sherman in 38; Thomas in 23–25
Michigan 5
Mill Springs, battle of 28
Missionary Ridge 29–31, *30*, 44–45, 109
Mississippi 45, 107

Mississippi River 5
Missouri 5, 56, 72
Mitchell, Joseph 15
Montgomery, Alabama 33
Morrison, Anna 90
Mosby's Men 111

N

Napoleon III (French emperor) 114
Nashville, battle of 32
North Carolina: Sherman advance on 48

O

Ohio 5
Orange Plank Road 98
Orange Turnpike 98

P

Patterson, Robert 27
Pemberton, John Clifford 43–44
Personal Memoirs (book by Sheridan) 115
Petersburg, siege of 13, 63, 110, 113
Pickett, George 12
Pickett's Charge 12, 129, *130*
Pittsburgh Landing 59
Pope, John 8–9, 76–77, 95–96, 125–126

R

Railroads 46, 59, 91, 110
Rapidan River 131
Rebel yell 93
Reconstruction 65, 115
Reed, Thomas Buchanan 112
Richmond, Virginia: burning of *132*; as Confederate capital 2; Seven Days' Battle and 7–8, 94–95; Sheridan raids near 104, 110
Richmond Examiner, The (newspaper) 7, 76
Richmond Whig, The (newspaper) 76
Ride Around McClellan *See* Stuart's Ride Around McClellan
Rienzi (horse) 112
Rochelle, James 22
Rock of Chickamauga *See* Thomas, George Henry
Rosecrans, William S. 28, 31
Rucker, Irene 115

S

St. Louis, Missouri 5
San Francisco, California 39
Santa Anna, Lopez de 24
Scott, Winfield 5, 6–7
secession: of Louisiana 40; of South Carolina 40; of Texas 6; of Virginia 1–2, 6–7, 123
Selma, Alabama 33
Seminole Indians 23, 89
Seminole Wars 37

137

Index

Seven Days' Battle 7–8, 75–76, 95
Seven Pines, battle of 75
Seymour, Bill 105
Shenandoah Valley: Jackson campaign
87, 90–94, 100; Lee campaign 7; Sheridan campaign 104, 111
Sheridan, John 104
Sheridan, Mary 104
Sheridan, Philip Henry vi, *103*, **103–118**,
113; at Beaver Dam 110; as cavalry commander 110; at Cedar Creek 112; chronology 117; death of 115; early career
of 105–106; early life of 104; as general-in-chief 115; historians on 116;
horsemanship of 104–105; Lee surrender witnessed by 114; at Missionary
Ridge 108–109; Petersburg besieged by
113; Reconstruction policies of 115;
Richmond raids led by 104, 110; Shenandoah campaign 104, 111–112; at Stones
River 107–108; Stuart defeated by 110,
131; in Texas 114–115; West Point training of 105
Sherman, John 37
Sherman, William Tecumseh v, *36*, **36–52**, *45*; Atlanta campaign of 32, 45–47,
63; banking career of 38; at Bull Run
(1861) 40; chronology 51; early career
of 37–38; early life of 37; as general of
the Army 49; Grant and 44, 60–61; historians on 50; in Kentucky 40–41; law career of 39; march to the sea of 47–48; in
Mexican War 38; at Missionary Ridge
30–31, 44–45; as secession foe 40; at Shiloh 42; on slavery 40; teaching career of
39–40; Thomas subordinated to 31;
Vicksburg besieged by 43–44; in victory
parade 49, 114; on war 36–37; West
Point training of 37
Shiloh, battle of 42, 59–61, *60*, 67
Simpson, Hannah 54
slavery iv, 6, 28, 40, 43, 48, 65, 122
Smith, E. Kirby 114
South Carolina 26, 38, 40, 48, 58, 73
states' rights iv, 6–7
Stones River, battle of 107–108
Stonewall Brigade 91, 93, 96, 98
Stuart, Archibald 120
Stuart, Jeb vi, *119*, **119–134**; at Antietam
126–127; at Brandy Station 128; John
Brown captured by 122–123; at Bull
Run (1861) 123–124; at Bull Run (1862)
125–126; cavalry favored by 121; chronology 133; death of (at Yellow Tavern)
110, 131; at Dranesville 124; early career
of 121–122; early life of 120–121; at Gettysburg 129–130; at Hazel Grove 127–
128; historians on 132; Jackson and
123; Lee and 124–125; West Point training of 121
Stuart's Ride Around McClellan
(Chickahominy Raid) 120, 124–125, 132
Suffolk Campaign 80

T

Taylor, Zachary 23–24, 72
Tennessee 27, 29–32, 42–46, 59–61, 81,
107–108
Texas 6, 23–24, 26, 56, 105–196, 114–115,
121
Thomas, Emory M. 132
Thomas, George Henry v–vi, *20*, **20–35**; at
Chickamauga 21, 29–30, 81; chronology
34; early career of 22–23; early life of
21–22; historians on 33; in Kentucky
27–28; in Mexican War 23–25; at Mill
Springs 28; at Missionary Ridge 30–31,
109; at Nashville 32–33; in San Francisco 26; West Point training of 22, 25
Traveler (horse) *10*
Twain, Mark 66–67

U

"Unconditional Surrender" 59
United States Military Academy at West
Point *See* West Point

V

Vicksburg, siege of 30, 43, 61–62, 67
Vigilantes 38
Virginia iv, 61; army of 7–11, 63–64, 70,
75, 78–81; Harper's Ferry raid 6, 122–
123; Richmond burning *132*; secession
of 1–2, 6–7, 123; Shenandoah campaign
87; Sheridan raids 104, 110–111
Virginia Military Institute 86, 89–90

W

Warrentown Pike 96
Washington, George 3, 4, 11, 14, 22, 62, 65
Washington, Martha 4
Washington and Lee University 14–15
West Point iv–v; Grant as student at 55–
56; Jackson as student at 88; Lee as student at 3–4; Lee as commandant of 5;
Longstreet as student at 71–72; Sheridan as student at 105; Sherman as student at 37; Stuart as student at 121;
Thomas as student at 22–23; Thomas as
instructor at 25
Wilderness, battle of the 13, 81, 98
Winchester (horse) 112

Y

Yakima Indians 106
Yates, Richard 58
Yellow Tavern, battle of 131

Z

Zollicoffer, Felix Kirk 28